LES PARSONS

Poetry
Themes &
Activities
Exploring the fun and fantasy of language

Pembroke Publishers Limited

© 1992 Pembroke Publishers Limited
528 Hood Road
Markham, Ontario
L3R 3K9

Published in the U.S.A. by
Heinemann Educational Books, Inc.
361 Hanover Street
Portsmouth, NH 03801-3959
ISBN (U.S.) 0-435-08730-4

Canadian Cataloguing in Publication Data

Parsons, Les, 1943-
  Poetry, themes, and activities

Includes bibliographical references and index.
ISBN 0-921217-76-5

1. Poetry – Study and teaching (Primary).
I. Title.

LB1527.P37 1992   372.64   C92-093089-1

Editor: Art Hughes
Design: John Zehethofer
Typesetting: Jay Tee Graphics Ltd.

Printed and bound in Canada
9 8 7 6 5 4 3 2 1

Contents

Foreword *5*

1. Setting the stage *7*
Why choose rhyming poetry? *7*
Why and how children respond to poetry *9*
When children write poetry *10*
Why teachers should write poetry for children *11*
Why use themes? *12*
How to use the themes *14*
  Theme starter *14*
  Activity palette *15*
  Theme resource list *16*

2. Adventures in color *17*
The Blue Song *18*
Activity palette *19*
  Creating a color-coded environment; developing word webs and related writing activities; exploring optical illusions; creating a photomontage or collage; interpreting color through dramatic play
Theme resource list *23*

3. Animals, animals, everywhere *25*
Midnight Zoo *26*
Cat's in the Cradle *28*
Activity palette *29*
  Sharing an animal finger play; sculpting with plasticine; creating egg-carton animals; making animal pop-ups; making lists and defining expressions; engaging in role play; responding through research
Theme resource list *32*

4. Hallowe'en and other spooky times *37*
Boooooooooo! *39*
Activity palette *40*
  Sculpting a monster world with plasticine; creating word webs; writing an acrostic 'story'; engaging in fairy tale role play; storytelling
Theme resource list *44*

5. All about me *47*
Why Can't I? *48*
Activity palette *50*
  Measuring 'me'; creating a photomontage or collage; making lists; sculpting self-portraits from plasticine; investigating through research
Theme resource list *55*

6 . In the city *59*
   Sounds of the City   60
   Activity palette   *62*
     Constructing a three-dimensional city; building with manipulative materials;
     comparing and categorizing characteristics; painting seasonal city pictures
   Theme resource list   *64*

7 . The world outside *67*
   The World Outside   68
   Activity palette   *69*
     Creating a learning centre; making mobiles of the outside world; exploring
     the neighborhood
   Theme resource list   *71*

8 . Imaginings *75*
   What If?   76
   Activity palette   *77*
     Storytelling through wordless books; writing in a variety of genres;
     imaginings in water; imaginings in sand
   Theme resource list   *79*

9 . ABCs and 1,2,3s *84*
   The 'Awful' ABCs   85
   Activity palette — alphabet   *87*
     Writing pattern books; sculpting letters with plasticine; responding through
     research; writing a picture book with a buddy
   Theme resource list — alphabet   *89*
   Numbers   91
   One Is a Pointer   92
   Activity palette — numbers   *94*
     Sharing a number finger play
   Theme resource-list — numbers   *93*

10 . Sound *96*
   Rock 'n' Roll Chant   97
   Activity palette   *99*
     Creating water-chime songs; making sound associations; categorizing
     sounds; cataloguing sounds; building a 'jug' band
   Theme resource list   *101*

11 . Setting up an activity-based environment *105*
   Based on beliefs   *106*
   Basic components   *106*
   Equipment checklist   *107*
   Learning centres   *107*

Index of activities   *110*

Glossary   *111*

Foreword

Poetry offers children priceless models of rich, heightened language from which they learn the true potential for language as a medium of thought, communication, and entertainment. Children are entranced by the rhythm and rhyme of poetry, intrigued by its metaphors, and attracted by its power to move them. Through rhythm and rhyme, they encounter the myths of their culture, learn their ABCs, and chant their skipping games. Through metaphor, concrete objects, acts, and events, almost magically, take on for children a larger-than-life dimension. Through poetry, words touch children across the spectrum of emotion, from the joy of laughter to the thrill of the unknown. As children develop their facility with language, they need to experience as much poetry as possible to understand the intrinsic nature of crafted, sculpted language.

In spite of poetry's many virtues and teachers' belief in those merits, poetry assumes, at best, only a minor role in primary programs. The underlying causes for this apparent neglect are fairly obvious. As the curriculum has expanded in size and complexity, so have the demands on the classroom teacher. A contemporary, child-centred, activity-based program requires countless extra hours to plan, implement, evaluate, renew, and maintain. As well, the trend toward school-based curriculum management places many added responsibilities on the shoulders of classroom teachers. Collaborating to improve instruction is certainly necessary and rewarding, but definitely time-consuming. Small wonder that classroom teachers can devote so little time to hunting down stimulating and useful poems in the daunting hodge-podge of library poetry sections.

Poetry, Themes, and Activities offers assistance in a number of ways. The selected poems are arranged in themes to match those widely in use in primary programs. The annotated, fully-referenced biblioraphies for each theme supply teachers with enough information to decide whether or not to use a particular poem and where to find it quickly if they do wish to use it. The poems were selected from books commonly available either in school or public libraries and include a blend of contemporary and traditional poets. The lists of suggested activities offer teachers a range of whole-learning experiences to help students explore and respond to the themes. Finally, the original poems in black-line master format with permission to photocopy ensure that teachers will have a fresh perspective for each theme and the flexibility to make use of these new poems as they see fit. In the rapid-fire, sophisticated world of contemporary education, *Poetry, Themes and Activities* is a practical and multidimensional tool for integrating poetry into any primary classroom program.

Acknowledgments

I would like to express my sincere appreciation to the children who responded to the original theme starter poems with the charming, free-spirited artwork featured in the book.

1. Setting the stage

Why choose rhyming poetry?

Almost all the poems in this collection rhyme. Free-form poetry, optic or concrete poetry, and the many kinds of pattern poems, such as cinquain and haiku, have been excluded deliberately. Overtly didactic poems have also been avoided. Many of the chosen poems are fanciful and some blatantly silly. And, while some may contain a serious intent, all are meant to be pleasing to the ear and, often, compellingly playful. Musicality, inventive imagery, and intriguing juxtapositions of the real and the make-believe were essential elements in the selection process. These criteria were established to match the interests and the needs of a specific audience. While there are many notable examples of poems that touch the heart and the mind without recourse to rhyme, this collection celebrates the song-like poems meant especially for young children. Besides, a casual browse through the primary poetry section of any library will reveal that most poetry written for young children does indeed rhyme — and for good reason.

Young children and adults differ significantly in what they think poetry is and how they expect poetry to operate. With adults, the form, or structure, of a poem grows out of its content or meaning. What a poem says often determines how it's said. Whether or not a poem rhymes, scans, or is set in lines and verses are characteristics that no longer dominate the genre or even form the criteria for judging a poem's worth. Instead, each poem is regarded as a unique creation defined by the intent and vision of the poet and judged by its intellectual and emotional impact.

As any parent or primary teacher can attest, children love to hear poems that sing with rhythm and rhyme, regardless of meaning. Stalwart infant poems are called nursery *rhymes*, after all, and illustrate the extent to which children will choose form over content without a qualm. Whatever relevance these ancient poems may have possessed has dimmed with time. Generations of children, however, continue to delight in such rhymes as "Hey, diddle diddle / The cat and the fiddle" and "Hickory, dickory, dock / The cat run up the clock" without worrying unduly about analyzing the text. Indeed, some children's poems were never meant to make sense. Consider the enduring appeal of a nonsense poem like "Jabberwocky." (" 'Twas brillig, and the slithy toves / Did gyre and gimble in the wabe. . . .)

Even worse, in adult eyes, is the child's refusal to discriminate between a finely-wrought poem and a piece of doggerel. In fact, the sillier or more nonsensical or grotesque the content appears to adults, the more a verse is apt to tickle the child's fancy, regardless of the roughness of the verse. To say that children's interests and humor are earthy is definitely understatement. "Burping," "bathroom," and "underwear" are perennial favorites in children's poetry. On the other hand, as children recursively construct their visions of reality, they start to differentiate between the real world and their imaginative, make-believe world. When presented with the juxtaposition of opposites, such as the real and the unreal, the known and the absurd, and the acceptable and the unacceptable, children are intrigued and amused. How else can one explain the enduring appeal of anonymous poems, such as the following, which are found in so many old 'treasuries' of children's verse?

> Ellen had a little bear
> To which she was so kind,
> And everywhere that Ellen went
> She had her bear behind.

If you're shaking your head in disapproval right now, you certainly aren't a child; if you're giggling uncontrollably, you're an unusual adult. For a child, the attractive components of this simple verse are unmistakable. The rhythm, rhyme, and situation echo a well-loved verse, "Mary Had a Little Lamb," the parody includes a play on words, and a hint of 'naughtiness' adds the spice of esoteric enjoyment.

Why and how children respond to poetry

How children and adults respond to and make use of poetry also differ dramatically. Since poetry, for adults, is a finely-honed vehicle for thought and feeling and a means by which they try to make sense of and cope with their lives, it tends to act as a catalyst for further reflection. In fact, the network of thoughts and feelings inspired by poetry often leads adults to read, write, think about, or discuss related issues in an attempt to deepen and extend their understanding. Young children, on the other hand, prefer to repeat and intensify the magic of the initial experience. If the poem is read aloud, they like to hear it over and over again and will often object to changes in delivery or any attempt to leave out verses. They also love to 'chime in' on the reading, clap their hands to the rhythm, mime facial expressions, act out events, or just copy out the words.

Not that this kind of exploration and sustained enjoyment of language is unknown to adults. Many adults take great delight in humming or singing along with a favorite song on the radio or even when sitting in a theatre. For some reason, singing while dancing to the music seems to heighten the enjoyment. If proficient on an instrument, they buy the sheet music and learn to play the song themselves. Some adults find themselves unconsciously 'conducting' a symphony and, in the theatre, any well-known Shakesperean soliloquy often turns into an inadvertent chorus as members of the audience mouth the words.

Children respond to poetry in varied but purposeful ways, even though those purposes may be unconscious from the child's point of view. The variety of their responses is closely linked to the manner in which they customarily explore their world. Children test out the characteristics of their environment through observation and manipulation. They aren't satisfied until they've examined an object from top to bottom and side to side over and over again. They like to see what happens when the object is dropped or rolled or covered in sand. They want to know if it has a smell or a taste, how hard or soft it is, and if all these characteristics are the same tomorrow as they are today. Children come to an understanding of the nature and parameters of the concrete world by examining individual elements over time from a variety of perspectives.

Similarly, as children explore the nature and parameters of language, poetry presents them with specific characteristics or elements not often found in their everyday experiences. Unlike concrete objects, however, the permanent characteristics of language are embedded in the flowing and shifting kaleidoscope of use. Intrinsically caught up in the network and patterns of everyday usage, children have difficulty developing and applying the perspective necessary to recognize the inherent principles that invest language with special power, grace, and beauty. Poetry, however, is crafted language. Its heightened nature lets children more easily experience and appreciate the qualities of language that affect listeners emotionally. Through a variety of responsive and manipulative activites, children interact with this significantly focused language and, in the process, revise their understanding of the potential of language itself.

When children write poetry

As young children investigate the metaphorical and metrical aspects of poetry, one avenue of response seems almost counterproductive. Even in the best of hands, rhyming poetry is difficult to create. When poets shape language to suit their purposes, they choose from a number of possible variations for the most penetrating or entertaining effect. With rhyme, however, there is an artistic trade-off because rhyme limits the number of choices for end-of-line words. On the other hand, rhyme and rhythm can imbue a work with essential energy and special qualities that facilitate the message, tone, or purpose. The skilful poet strikes a delicate balance between the benefits of rhyme and rhythm and the limitations of these conventions. When the perfect balance is found, the words and rhythms seem natural, spontaneous, and true.

Young children, on the other hand, possess an extremely limited vocabulary compared with that of the poets they read and to whom they listen. At a time when they should be expanding their use of language to match the growing complexity of their language needs, the writing of rhyming poetry presents them with an anomaly. The very language that delights them most is the most difficult in which to communicate. Limited choice in vocabulary inevitably forces children to substitute invented words or to sacrifice the sense or complexity of the content. In the case of rhyme, the form overwhelms the content. Generally speaking, whatever poetry writing they attempt usually results in the creation of doggerel.

At some point, children will either try to emulate this kind of crafted language or develop the reservoir of language necessary to make the results more satisfying. If children want to write poetry, they should. When children are ready to try, they will. The choice is theirs. Writing a poem, however, is only one narrow band on the spectrum of enriching responses to the world of poetry. With the activities in this book, children are encouraged to find alternate ways in which to revel in, appreciate, and learn from this special brand of language.

Why teachers should write poetry for children

The evolution and popularity of 'rap' music forced many people to re-examine their attitudes toward poetry. For some reason, the word 'poet' possessed an esoteric, almost mystical quality. People mistakenly assumed that poets were removed from mainstream society by vision, craft, and life experiences. Regardless of who they are or what they do for a living, poets are people who choose to reflect on and communicate their sense of themselves and the human experience through poetry. Obviously, they need to observe that experience close at hand. With 'rap' music, the link between poet and audience is direct and interdependent. These poets spring from and speak for the very audiences that come to hear them.

In the case of children's poetry, the link between poet and audience is even more immediate and interdependent. A poet writing for children attempts to share an understanding of and perspective on experience as gained through the sensibilities of a child. No one can write for children with that kind of sensibility without direct exposure to children. Poets draw on their own childhood memories, certainly, but those memories have to be rediscovered, re-examined, clarified, and distilled through observation of real children. No wonder the experiences of parenting and teaching have been the source of so many children's poems.

Many teachers have never tried to write poetry because they

think that they aren't qualified. As 'rap' music also so clearly demonstrated, poetry is for everyone and anyone can write poetry. If teachers don't write for children, then who should? Who knows more about that specific audience of children than they do? Who knows more about their mode of language, the way they perceive the world, and the things that are important to them? Rather than special knowledge of metre or sophisticated vocabulary, a person writing for children needs an understanding of children and the will to communicate with them. With honesty, patience, some craft, and a little time, any teacher can write poetry that will touch, charm, and entertain children.

By the same token, the investment of time is a significant hurdle. Is writing poetry sufficiently worthwhile to justify the outlay of precious time? Actually, teachers can't afford not to write poetry. The concept that writing poetry is a vital, commonplace, and accepted activity can't be taught. It can only be modeled. The value of risk-taking, of offering your words for others to share, of entering into a collaborative community of writers also can only be passed on through example. In so many ways, the simple act of writing for children creates an experiential model from which they can extract essential ideas about what language is, what it's for, and how it's used.

The most compelling reason for teachers to write poetry for their students is also the most selfish. Writing poetry for children is fun. Teachers get to rediscover and enjoy the world through a child's wondering eyes. They get to revisit treasured memories of people, places, objects, and events. Vicariously, they get to think and act like a child all over again. Besides, teachers will never have a more generous, responsive, and appreciative audience than the children in their own classroom. The first time they craft a poem, present it to their children, and witness as the words thrill and move them, they will be hooked for life. Why should teachers write poetry for children? Quite simply, there's too much joy in the experience not to.

Why use themes?

The three components of this collection were developed to satisfy the needs of busy classroom teachers. *The author's original poems* provide fresh stimulation and the opportunity to photocopy at will; the *annotated bibliographies* assist teachers with the tasks of finding and choosing appropriate material; and the *activity lists* suggest a variety of ways in which children can respond to and explore the selected poems. At the same time, the collection is consciously organized into themes to ensure that children's exposure to poetry becomes an integral part of their current learning/teaching environments.

Teachers of young children already use themes widely. In fact, they commonly organize cross-curricular units on the basis of themes. By selecting a particular topic and using that focus to integrate all aspects of their program, teachers encourage, support, and reinforce children's learning. From the point of view of the child, reading, writing, listening, speaking, viewing, and representing are all inherent aspects of the same process. Children themselves see no differences among language-based activities and intrinsically employ visual arts, dramatic arts, and manipulation of materials for similar purposes. The use of themes, then, mirrors the integrated nature of learning. In this sense, whole language becomes an integral part of whole learning.

Since children's inherent predilection is toward an integrated approach to learning, the use of themes allows them more easily to use their understanding in one area of the program to unlock and further develop their understanding in another. Each additional, related experience tends to mature, deepen, and reinforce insights previously gained. A simple example would be the study of animals. A teacher obviously would have to subdivide such a general theme into smaller, more manageable topics, such as farm animals or zoo animals.

The following activities illustrate a few obvious possibilities for a unit on farm animals:

- visiting a petting farm
- singing animal songs
- reading aloud and independent reading from a range of genre, such as exposition, storybooks, and poetry
- creating cooperative chart stories
- writing stories based on actual experiences and imagined situations
- picture-making of all kinds
- sculpting in plasticine or clay
- role-playing situations in which farm animals are cared for

- developing story theatre from a favorite story, such as "The Three Billy Goats Gruff" or "The Three Little Pigs"
- building a farm in the sand centre
- recreating a farmyard pond at the water centre

By choosing themes that reflect the interests of most young people and ensuring that the activities are open-ended and sufficiently individualized to accommodate the children's natural, developmental ranges, teachers can modify and manipulate their learning/teaching environments to maximize learning opportunities. The sole purpose of a thematic approach is to organize and facilitate learning. *The theme is a means to an end* and must never become an end in itself.

With poetry organized into common teaching themes, the theme gains another perspective and a deeper potential. Just as important, since comprehension is so closely aligned with experience, exposure to other aspects of the theme allows children to bring a larger experiential background and a heightened sense of understanding to the particular qualities of the poetry. Organized by theme, poetry complements the learning and the learning heightens the appreciation of the poetry. Naturally, a child-centred, activity-based learning/teaching environment requires considerable planning and preparation. For a more detailed guide, see chapter 11, "Setting up an activity-based environment."

How to use the themes

Each theme has three components:

- *Theme starter*
- *Activity palette*
- *Theme resource list*

While the themes can be used on their own, the separate components can be easily integrated with a teacher's existing unit to extend and enrich that topic. Following is a brief explanation of each component along with suggestions for implementation.

Theme starter
Each theme begins with a new, original poem. Flexibility is the key, however. While these poems can readily initiate the unit

and lead into making use of some of the activities and resources suggested for each theme, they can also be used in other ways. Many teachers are familiar with these themes and may already have their own favorite approaches to introducing them. As well, the particular dynamic of a class or a teacher's previous experience with a group of children may suggest other alternatives. After looking over the *activity palette* and the *theme resource list*, teachers can decide for themselves how best to start.

What the theme starter does is ensure a fresh ingredient for children and teachers alike, regardless of a theme's familiarity. As well, copyright considerations often restrict how poems are used in a classroom. In black-line master format and with permission already granted, these poems can be duplicated for multiple copies or easily transferred to acetate sheets for use on an overhead projector, again adding to the flexibility of the unit. Suggestions are included for introducing each poem and following up on its special qualities or features.

Activity palette

The activities in this section should be used much as an artist uses the colors arrayed on a painter's palette. Depending on the needs, interests, and previous experiences of a particular group of children, a teacher will pick and choose among the activities listed. Whether an activity is matched with the *theme starter* poem, one of the poems listed in the *theme resource list*, a resource of the teacher's own choosing, or even used at all depends on the teacher's professional judgment. One teacher may decide that a particular activity forms an effective initiating experience for the entire theme, while another may hold back that activity until the close of the unit.

The *activity palette* also presents teachers with a broad range of activities from which to choose. Visual arts, small-group discussions, choral speaking, role-playing, and sand and water experimentation are just some of the suggested experiences through which children can explore the ideas and language contained in the selected poems. While children will have many opportunities to use written language to record ideas, observations, and questions, make lists, plan a process, and organize information, they will *not* be asked to create poems themselves. The creation of original rhyming poems is best left to the language development of individual children. On the other hand, as children themselves choose to respond this way, they should be encouraged and assisted in every way possible. Teachers can also personalize, individualize, and extend the unit by adding their own activities.

Theme resource list

Based on the criteria detailed in this chapter, several poems dealing with different aspects of each theme have been selected to form the basis of the unit. Each poem is annotated, and the description includes a brief excerpt and bibliographic information. From these references, teachers can gain an overview of the content, tone, and chief characteristics of each poem, decide whether or not a particular poem suits their needs, and, if desired, know where to find it. A balance between traditional and more recent favorites and between established and lesser-known poets blends accessibility with freshness and variety. Whatever experience teachers have had with poetry, they should find something useful in these listings. The listings, however, are by no means comprehensive. As with *activity palettes*, teachers can tailor the unit by adding their personal favorites and discoveries.

2. *Adventures in color*

This theme blends recognition of the basic colors and an examination of color in the natural world with emotions associated with color. The *activity palette* describes a number of specific activities and lists the materials required for each. As the theme builds, however, just having a variety of media and colorful materials at hand will allow children to take the initiative. Materials that may suggest picture-making to some children may encourage others to experiment with blending and shading. In this case, the medium really is the message. The special characteristics, capabilities, colors, or even textures of various visual arts and manipulative materials will, of themselves, stimulate children to explore and respond to color in their own special ways.

Some of the resources at hand could include the following in various colors:

poster paints
wax or pencil crayons
felt markers
plasticine
construction paper
manipulative materials,
   such as colored Lego

oil pastels
chalk or chalk pastels
writing paper
pipe cleaners
'found' materials
'dress-up' materials

Theme starter: "The Blue Song"

Before reading "The Blue Song" aloud, teachers may suggest that children listen for the different kinds of blue things in the poem and think about how the poem makes them feel in the

The Blue Song

Blueberry pie
A clear-blue sky
A brand-new pair of jeans

Batman's cape
A kind of grape
And steel-blue submarines

Blue is free
And what I see
When a bluebird flies so high

But when I'm blue
There's nothing to do
But sit by myself and cry

different stanzas and why they feel as they do. Young children are often ambivalent about the ending of this poem. They enjoy the rhyme and rhythm and the sense of completion, but feel the sadness in a direct and, sometimes, unsettling way.

Follow-up suggestions for "The Blue Song"

• As children suggest blue things not mentioned in the poem, the teacher records them on chart paper or on the chalkboard under the title "Another Blue Song." Rhymes should neither be requested nor rejected. The results can be read aloud in a variety of ways. The author of each line can be invited to read that line as it comes up in the free-verse poem, volunteers can be solicited for each line, or the entire poem can be read in choral fashion.

• After another color is chosen, the teacher heads up a piece of chart paper with the appropriate title, such as "The Red Song." Again, the children's suggestions are recorded and read aloud.

Activity palette

• *Creating a color-coded environment*
The entire environment in an activity-oriented classroom can be keyed to the exploration of color. Teachers can set up a 'color' table. Each day, children bring in objects of a designated color for discussion, and display them on the table. Children who have articles of clothing of that color can be encouraged to wear them that day. Colored manipulative materials, such as plasticine, pipe cleaners, wool, or fabric, can be included. Food coloring can be added to the water table. Activities at the paint and drawing centres can also be directed to specific colors. In this way, the classroom itself is transformed into an artist's palette.

• *Developing word webs and related writing activities*
Depending on their age and experience, children can work on this activity independently, in small groups, or in a large group under the direction of the teacher. On chart paper, a word web of colors is developed from the source word.

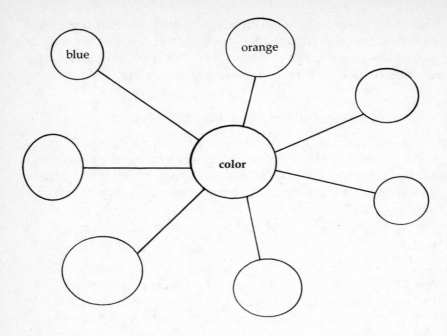

• A color extracted from the wheel can become the focal point of a new word web. Children should be encouraged to include words that they associate with that color as well as objects that are ordinarily that color, for example, "hot" for the color red.

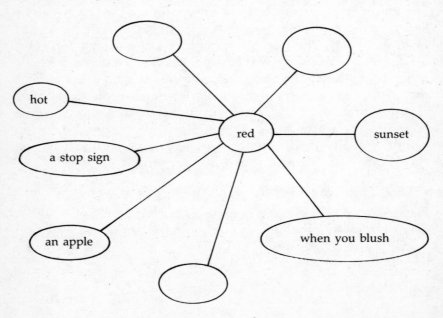

This is an ideal activity for small groups. Each group is given a large sheet of construction paper the same color as the source color and a magic marker. One child is designated as scribe. The small-group charts can later be shared with the large group.

• In another approach, individuals are given a sheet of construction paper in the color of their choice. They cover the surface with words, phrases, and drawings stimulated by that color.

• The various charts can be used for a classification activity. Children are asked to group words and phrases from the charts according to what they have in common, for example, "all the feelings or things I use."

• In another follow-up activity individuals take a word from one of the charts and make associations from their own experiences, for example, "things that make me blush" or "what I know about sunsets."

• *Exploring optical illusions*
Baum, Arlene and Joseph Baum. *Opt, an Illusionary Tale*. New York: Viking Penguin, 1987.

In this excellent resource book, a jester leads children through the Kingdom of Opt, a land of optical illusions. In one trick, children stare at a red balloon with a white balloon beside it. After 30 seconds, the white balloon turns green. Each illusion is explained, and suggestions are given for creating additional ones. This book makes an intriguing component for any study of color.

• *Creating a photomontage or collage*
From magazines, children cut out and paste pictures, words, and phrases associated with the color of their choice. They can be encouraged to blend and overlap pictures for unusual and interesting effects and to keep the total surface area balanced with the size, type, and shapes of the cutouts they choose. Some children may want to try two or three colors in the same creation.

• *Interpreting color through dramatic play*
Children are asked to show with their faces and bodies what a particular color looks and feels like. If space allows, they can be encouraged to move around as the color dictates. The directions to the children could be similar to the following: "Use your whole

Adventures in black

Ian (age 7)

Christopher (age 8)

body and your facial expressions to show what red is like. What does red look like? How does it feel? When I ask you to move, remember that you must not touch anyone else or any object in the room. Now move around the room as though you are the color red.''

Theme resource list

• Ciardi, John. *Fast and Slow*. Illustrated by Becky Grove. Boston: Houghton Mifflin, 1975.

"Why the Sky Is Blue." These charming, rhyming couplets explain where all the other colors went and why blue was the only color left for the sky. In the case of red, for example, we're told that the "sunsets, of course, take out the red / And pour it into the ocean bed."

• Merriam, Eve. *Blackberry Ink*. Illustrated by Hans Wilhelm. New York: William Morrow, 1985.

"Berries on the Bushes." Eve Merriam chooses delicate, color-filled details and gently paints a portrait of a simple, lovely experience. Children enjoy the pleasure of picking berries. "In the summer sun / Bring along a bucket / And pluck every one."

• O'Neil, Mary. *Hailstones and Halibut Bones: Adventures in Color*. Illustrated by John Wallner. New York: Doubleday, 1989.

This new edition does full justice to a children's classic. The rhymes, images, and perceptions are as fresh and refreshing as they were when the book was first published 30 years ago. Poems about purple, gold, black, brown, blue, gray, white, orange, red, pink, green, and yellow are included. A few samples follow:

"What Is Purple?" If you had any doubts about the importance of purple, this poem assures us that "It's sort of a great / Grand-mother to pink." From time to flowers to jam to feelings, purple is turned inside out in tasteful, rollicking rhymes.

"What Is Black?" The pinpoint details pile up one on top of another in a delightful mosaic of places, things, animals, sounds, and feelings. Content and form are intrinsically joined.

Each poem offers similar revelations and delicate, natural phrasings.

• Silverstein, Shel. *Where the Sidewalk Ends*. New York: Harper and Row, 1974.

"Colors." What color are people? In this short but intriguing poem, Shel Silverstein offers a possible answer. "My skin is kind of sort of brownish / Pinkish yellowish white" he begins and then says that his "eyes are greyish blueish green" that look "orange in the night." And what color are people on the inside? The ending answers that question, as well, in a mystical, illuminating way.

Looking back

Keeping a photographic record is a useful practice during any thematic unit. Experiences with role-playing and choral speaking, for example, can be recalled more readily when prompted by a photograph or two. Since color is the core of this unit, creating a photo album of the unit's activities is a natural, culminating activity. As well as the pictures taken during the course of the unit, children can also choose among their media creations for a favorite to be photographed. Through group discussion or by assigning pages to individuals or pairs, captions can be written for each photograph. Prominently displayed, the album can be read and enjoyed all year.

3. Animals, animals, everywhere

Few themes are as deeply rooted in children's immediate experiences and emerging interests as animals. Many children have already encountered such family pets as cats, dogs, birds, turtles, or fish. A surprising number have had direct experience with such wildlife creatures as squirrels, raccoons, or foxes. Some have already begun a life-long love of zoos, the circus, and conservation parkland.

Animals also figure prominently in children's pre-school culture. Young children have been taught rhymes ("This Little Piggy Went to Market" and "Baa Baa Black Sheep"), read tales ("Goldilocks and the Three Bears" and "The Ugly Duckling"), and sung songs about animals ("Old McDonald Had a Farm" and "There Was an Old Woman Who Swallowed a Fly"). With this background, it's not surprising that the literature and reference materials written for young children are rich in animal themes and that primary school curricula and excursions inevitably focus on the study of animals.

With an abundance of material from which to choose and children's ever-burgeoning interest in the animal world, teachers face the enviable tasks of deciding how to subdivide this theme for greater effectiveness and how to cull the best material from the vast quantity available. The selections and activities that follow should help with both tasks.

Theme starter: "Midnight Zoo"

This behind-the-scenes fantasy of a zoo at night describes what happens when the humans go home. Children are intrigued and

Midnight Zoo

On a certain, silly, summer night
(The moon was burning blue),
The lion roared,
"Come out! I'm bored"
One midnight at the zoo.

From shadowed cages everywhere,
They slithered, hopped, and flew,
As three baboons
Blew up balloons
One midnight at the zoo.

Then a hippo passed out popcorn,
As a penguin played kazoo,
And a rattlesnake
Served peppermint cake
One midnight at the zoo.

An elephant and a parakeet danced
With a bashful kangaroo,
And the rhino's mum
Chewed bubblegum
One midnight at the zoo.

But the lion finally yawned and said,
"I'm afraid the party's through.
The night is done.
I see the sun.
It's morning at the zoo."

Back to their cages every one,
They slithered, hopped, and flew.
But they'd come again
Next midnight when
The summer moon burned blue!

amused by the vivid word pictures, attracted by the regal attitude of the lion, and attentive to the repetition in the rhyme scheme. The hint of mystery and the supernatural adds spice to the fun. Before reading the poem aloud, suggest that, when you finish, volunteers recount the scene or image they enjoyed most as they listened.

Follow-up suggestions for "Midnight Zoo"

• Role-playing evolves naturally from the context and format of this poem. To start, assign a volunteer to portray the lion at the beginning of the poem, "Come out! I'm bored." The teacher in role portrays another animal and engages the lion in conversation.

Through discussion afterward, children can explore the characteristics each animal displayed and then move on to suggest the characteristics other animals in the poem might possess. When the students are comfortable with the concept, several at a time can be assigned roles and the scene can be replayed.

• The poem is rich in unusual and amusing word pictures. In the medium of their choice, children can recreate visually their favorite scene. The scene can then be labeled either with the appropriate line(s) from the poem or with a child's own description of the scene.

Activity palette

• *Sharing an animal finger play*
Finger play has always been popular with children and with their parents. Many parents have delighted in performing the age-old rhyme

> "This is the church.
> Here is the steeple.
> Open the doors.
> Here are the people."

Children's fascination with finger play seems directly related to the tactile manner in which they explore their world. Through finger play, the concrete expression of abstract concepts is literally at their finger tips.

Cat's in the Cradle

Cat's in the cradle
(Cup hands for cradle)
Bird's on the wing
(Join hands at thumbs. Flutter hands.)
Tiger's in the jungle
(Separate hands and curve fingers into claws.)
Ready to spring
(Thrust hands/claws toward audience.)
Cow's in the milk shed
(Both hands make a milking motion.)
Goldfish in the bowl
(One hand makes a fish-like, swimming movement.)
Rabbit slowly sinks
(One fist is the rabbit's head, with index and second
finger extended for the ears.)
Down its rabbit hole
(Curve one arm in front to represent ground level
and let 'rabbit' slowly sink down behind.)

Response to "Midnight Zoo"

Jeff (age 7)

James (age 8)

Response to "Midnight Zoo"

Ashley (age 7)

Jenny (age 7)

Natasha (age 7)

Crystal (age 7)

Justin (age 7)

Amy (age 7)

Dwayne (age 7)

Patrick (age 7)

- *Sculpting with plasticine*

Two unique reference books can direct and enhance children's use of plasticine. A description of each and how they might be used in this unit follows:

Reid, Barbara. *Playing with Plasticine.* Toronto: Kids Can Press, 1988.

Beginning with some background information on plasticine and tips on how to develop a number of basic shapes, this unique reference book goes on to offer step-by-step instructions on how to build and explore an imaginative plasticine universe that includes everything from bugs, birds, and beasts to planets and stars.

The chapter entitled *Bugs, Birds, and Beasts* starts with simple animal shapes and then presents instructions on how to create an entire menagerie of creatures from plasticine. Snakes, bugs, lizards, cats, dogs, mice, pigs, and elephants are just some of the many animals included in the chapter. Although the basic shapes and characteristics are built up step by step, children are encouraged to adapt, invent, and make the creations their own.

Have You Seen Birds? (written by Joanne Oppenheim and illustrated by Barbara Reid) is an ideal extension of the sculpting activities begun in *Playing with Plasticine.* (See page 35 for a description.) Children should be encouraged to choose a subject in the animal kingdom from some group other than birds. The book will provide them with a variety of stimulating new ways to manipulate this medium. Since the examples from the book use colored plasticine, having different colors available will facilitate the success of this activity.

- *Creating egg-carton animals*

Haas, Rudi and Hans Blohm. *Egg-Carton Zoo.* Toronto: Oxford University Press, 1986.

Guaranteed to complement any unit on animals, this book advocates easy-to-find, sensible materials in a simple-to-use, inspiring style. Inside every plain egg carton is a fantastic menagerie of animals just waiting to be released. This book shows you how to do it. The directions for making each creature are supplied by large, wordless photographs, easy for children of all ages to follow, and are accompanied by pertinent background information. The animals described in this way are frogs, water birds, pigs, butterflies, turtles, bears, leopards, whales, zebra, deer, weasels, dogs, elephants, walrus, chameleons, mice, and dinosaurs. The book closes with an appeal for children to open their imaginations and free the wondrous, fantasy animals within.

• *Making animal pop-ups*
Irvine, Joan. *How to Make Pop-ups.* Illustrated by Barbara Reid. Toronto: Kids Can Press, 1987.

For children of all ages, pop-up books possess a special, magical appeal. When a two-dimensional storybook is imbued with three-dimensional characteristics, it takes on an added layer of reality and a unique life of its own. This added dimension makes the mixture especially powerful when explored by young, emergent readers. *How to Make Pop-ups* puts this power into children's hands and allows them to create their own pop-up books.

The techniques are ingenious and surprisingly simple, the directions straightforward and clear, and the illustrations clarifying and supportive. A world of pop-up frogs, butterflies, bears, fish, rabbits, and dragons awaits. The directions are easy to follow and inspirational. The book works!

• *Making lists and defining expressions*
The English language is rich in animal metaphors. In small groups with a designated scribe or in a large group directed by the teacher, children first develop a list on chart paper of all the animal expressions they can remember. By offering a few examples, such as ''I'm hungry as a bear'' or ''It's raining cats and dogs,'' the teacher can 'seed' the list-making.

In the second half of the activity, children offer an explanation or definition of each expression. This activity works best and comprehension is maximized when the teacher accepts the children's own language and encourages a variety of possible phrasings.

• *Engaging in role play*
Children can be encouraged to display, process, and communicate what they know of animal characteristics through simple role play. Either as an introduction to a poem about a specific

animal or as a follow-up, children can use facial expressions and their bodies to portray that animal. They can move around the classroom as that animal might move (without, of course, interfering with anyone else) and make the appropriate vocal sounds.

In another variation, children can choose any animal they wish. With or without vocal sounds, they can portray that animal, one by one, as the rest of the class guesses the animal's identity. As a wrap-up to this variation, all the children can move around the room, in role, as any animal they've seen portrayed.

• *Responding through research*
Farris, Katherine. *The Kids' Question and Answer Book*. Toronto: Greey de Pencier Books, 1987.

Complete with full-color photographs and illustrations, this fascinating compendium of children's questions and the answers to those questions is an invaluable addition to any animal theme. Sample a few of the questions and see if you wouldn't like to know the answers, let alone the children in your classroom.

Why don't birds fall off branches when they sleep?
Why do bats hang upside down?
Why do cats have whiskers?

Hundreds of these questions and the answers await in this soft-cover, attractive volume.

Theme resource list

• Cole, Joanna, ed. *A New Treasury of Children's Poetry*. New York: Doubleday, 1984.

"Eletelephony" by Laura E. Richards. Children delight in the comical central image and the inventive word play in the story of an elephant "Who tried to use the telephant- / No! No! I mean an elephone." The increasingly tangled language neatly captures the tangled visual image.

"Mice" by Rose Fyleman. What animal unit could be complete without the familiar strains of "I think mice / Are rather nice"? The language is simple and direct, the rhymes are tasteful, and the off-handed irony is delicious. "Mice" is an enduring, delightful, choral-speaking favorite.

• Fargeon, Eleanor. *Eleanor Fargeon's Poems for Children.* New York: J.B. Lippincott, 1951.

"Cat." All you need to hear is "Cat! Scat! After her, after her. . ." and you will probably find that warm, personal memories of this poem come flooding back. Filled with a rollicking, raucous rhythm and sound effects galore, "Cat" is another perennial choice for choral speaking.

• Foster, John, ed. *A First Poetry Book.* New York: Oxford University Press, 1985.

"The Frog's Lament" by Aileen Fisher. "I can't bite / like a dog" begins this clever lament. In the process of complaining about what it can't do, the frog identifies a host of protective characteristics that other animals possess. The rhymes are embedded in natural, everyday language and flow spontaneously from the content.

• Greenfield, Eloise. *Under the Sunday Tree.* Paintings by Amos Ferguson. New York: Harper and Row, 1988.

"To Catch a Fish." Accompanied by a distinctive painting of children fishing, "To Catch a Fish" contains a wonderful blend of content and form in which the exact word needed to express the meaning just happens to rhyme. As anyone who has fished will recognize, "you add the bait / you concentrate / and then you wait / you wait   you wait."

• Hall, Donald, ed. *The Oxford Book of Children's Verse in America.* New York: Oxford University Press, 1985.

"Combination" by Mary Ann Hoberman. The first stanza begins, "A flea flew by a bee." With six stanzas all together, how could any child (or teacher) resist trying out this "Combination"? A teacher doesn't need to 'do' anything with this poem. It will 'do' itself.

• Heidbreder, Robert. *Don't Eat Spiders.* Illustrated by Karen Patkau. Toronto: Oxford University Press, 1985.

"A Big Bare Bear." What would you expect from a poem that begins, "A big bare bear / bought a bear balloon / For a big bear trip / to the bare, bare moon" and that ends with ". . . on his big bum bum''? Although it may not be your personal cup of tea, expect your children to request it over and over again.

"Don't Eat Spiders". As soon as you warn children, "Don't eat spiders / Even in play / Fried or mashed / Or in any way. . .", you have captured their total attention and the laughter starts bubbling up. Add a lot of 'gross', childlike details and the recipe has to be a winner.

• Moore, Lilian. *See My Lovely Poison Ivy*. New York: Atheneum, 1977.

"Whoo?" An owl and the wind shriek back and forth in this simple but entertaining sound-effects poem. The call "whooooooo" and the answer "wheeeeee" echo through the verses, leading children to spontaneously join right in.

• Oppenheim, Joanne. *Have You Seen Birds?* Illustrated by Barbara Reid. Richmond Hill, Ontario: Scholastic Canada, 1986.

A kaleidoscopic array of birds is revealed in a unique and vivid format. Details spill out in rhythmical, compelling questions, such as "Have you heard town birds? / Rapping-at-the-bark birds, / Cooing-in-the-park birds." The engaging verses are accompanied by photographs of intricate, colorful, plasticine models in appropriate settings. The artist's skilful use of this children's medium evokes special interest and a natural desire to respond to the poems in kind.

• Silverstein, Shel. *Where the Sidewalk Ends*. New York: Harper and Row, 1974.

"Boa Constrictor." Years ago, the folk group "Peter, Paul, and Mary" made this lyric famous with their in-concert, fun-filled treatment. Simply told, the narrator of the poem describes the progress of a boa constrictor as it swallows a toe and moves on up to the narrator's head. The poem is ripe for a number of choral effects. The audience, for example, can echo the narrator.
    Narrator: Well, what do you know?
    Audience: What do you know?
    Narrator: It's nibbling my toe.
    Audience: It's nibbling my toe!
    The pace can be increased, making the mood more frantic as the boa constrictor moves up from toe to neck.

"The Silver Fish." A lovely silver fish offers his young captor a wish in exchange for freedom. The fish asks him if he'll choose a "kingdom of wisdom? A palace of gold? / Or all the fancies your mind can hold?" Guess again! This familiar, fairy tale pattern is turned upside down by Shel Silverstein's wonderfully warped and novel mind. The ending is exquisite.

Looking back

Throughout this unit, one type of animal is mentioned again and again. Children's experiences with their pets keep popping up in discussions, drawings, writings, preferred story books, and the myriad other activities stimulated by an animal theme. Some teachers like to augment these vicarious experiences with actual pet visits to the classroom.

Successful and safe visits require careful planning, some essential investigation, and a few, simple rules. Some school boards have strict regulations about animals in the classroom. Dogs, for example, are often allowed only from recognized organizations. Turtles, as well, are often suspect because of disease. Information about allergies among the children also needs to be gathered and considered. In all cases, school principals should be consulted before the visits are organized. An adult from home to accompany each pet should be a prerequisite, and only a few pets each day should be introduced. All these precautions are richly rewarded when children can share with others the actual experience of a valued and specific, animal friend.

4. Hallowe'en and other spooky times

Peek-a-boo is one of the earliest games parents play with their children. People delightfully disappear and reappear before anxiety has a chance to build. The effectiveness of the game rests on the fact that, in a child's universe, anything is possible. Through experience, the known world widens: dirt tastes terrible, a fall can hurt, and the cat doesn't like its tail being pulled. On the other hand, the unknown possibilities seem countless and lurk unsettlingly near.

Experiencing some of these possibilities can be exciting as well as frightening. As a child gets older, the game of peek-a-boo turns into "Boo! Scared you, didn't I?" The thrill of exploring the bounds of the known and the safe carries with it a sense of danger. When being tossed into the air from a parent's arms becomes tame, children turn to faster and faster merry-go-rounds, ferris wheels, and the dreaded roller coasters. At the same time, the world of nighttime, darkness, and shadows becomes tinged with a touch of menace. Unknown possibilities might also be malevolent. Just the title of Judith Viorst's classic depiction of childhood fears reveals much about the dark side of this childhood world. Her book is called *My Mama Says There Aren't Any Zombies, Ghosts, Vampires, Creatures, Demons, Monsters, Fiends, Goblins, or Things* (New York: Macmillan, 1973). As in the book, children need reassurance that the world of their nightmares truly is benign. Although a vampire inhabits Sesame Street, he is obsessed only with counting and the rest of the so-called monsters are kindly, cuddly, child-loving creatures, even irrascible Oscar.

This unit explores the benevolent, fun-filled aspects of exploring the unknown, from the traditional rituals of a child's

Hallowe'en to the mysteries encountered in the shadows of a child's imagination. As every teacher of primary children knows, except for the almost unbearable wait for Christmas, the breathless anticipation, excitement, and fun associated with Hallowe'en is an unmatched experience in children's lives. The poetry that follows will complement the roster of activities teachers have already devised to turn this cultural stimulus into an enriching learning opportunity.

Theme starter: "Booooooooo!"

The following poem highlights the ambivalence children feel toward frightening experiences. In short, rhyming couplets, a collection of scary, stereotypical sights, sounds, and images unfurl in rapid succession. The tone, however, remains playful and the ending overtly restores the proper perspective. The poem works best when read aloud with a breathless, 'campy' delivery. Encourage the children to predict what the second rhyme will be in each couplet and to say their guesses aloud, in chorus with you, as you read.

Response to "Booooooooo!"

Nelly (age 7)

Booooooooo!

I love. . .
                a just right
                stormy night
                shutters banging
                webs hanging
                doors squeaking
                floors creaking
                goose-bumping
                strange thumping
                candles flickering
                witches snickering
                groans and moans
                and bunches of bones
                shadows creeping
                lightning leaping
                bats flying
                ghosts sighing
                ghouls mumbling
                castles crumbling
                a scary ending. . .

                        but just pretending!

Follow-up suggestions for "Booooooooo!"

• Make an overhead transparency of the poem or print the poem on chart paper. Ask the children to read aloud the second line of each rhyming couplet with you as you read the poem again. Point to their lines as you read. In another variation, children can point to and read aloud their favorite line or couplet.

• Once the poem has become familiar enough, it's a natural for choral reading. The first and last line can be read by everyone. Individual lines or couplets can be assigned to volunteers. Sound effects can be added by other volunteers. A large piece of stiff cardboard, for example, can be shaken vigorously to approximate thunder. A wealth of other sighing, moaning, snickering, thumping, or creaking noises can be added to taste.

Activity palette

• *Sculpting a monster world with plasticine*
Reid, Barbara. *Playing with Plasticine.* Toronto: Kids Can Press, 1988.

In the chapter entitled "A Whole Bunch of Stuff" children are encouraged to use their favorite plasticine techniques to create their own monsters. They are then challenged to invent a whole monster world, from pets to a monster bathroom to a monster teacher. Since monsters are creatures of the imagination, this open-ended activity lets children give free rein to their inventive impulses without worrying unduly about verisimilitude or whether or not their creatures 'look real'. This activity is ideal for a collaborative project for small or large groups. For a full description of the contents and organization of Barbara Reid's book, see chapter 3, "Animals, animals, everywhere."

• *Creating word webs*
Teachers can capitalize on the prior experience and rich language that children bring to this theme. With word webs, children can organize and share their knowledge and then use the common reservoir of language to articulate and communicate their own ideas and thoughts.

Depending on their age and experience, children can work on

this activity independently, in small groups, or in a large group under the direction of the teacher. On chart paper, a web of related words is developed from the source word.

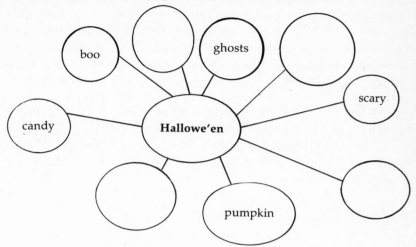

• Words can be extracted from the web by individuals or groups and separate webs developed around those focal words. Children should be encouraged to use phrases, if they desire, and to extend their choices to words that describe feelings or moods. These webs can act as a source of core vocabulary as children create labels, lists, or stories in the course of the unit.

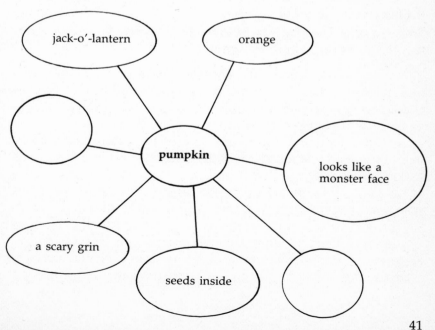

- *Writing an acrostic 'story'*

Lewis Carrol popularized acrostic poetry. (The name comes from the Greek *akros*, "tip" and *stichos*, "row.") In this special kind of language puzzle, a word is written vertically down the left-hand margin of the paper. Each line then starts with a word beginning with the designated letter. An acrostic poem does not necessarily have to rhyme. Since their experience is almost entirely with rhyming poetry, children often find the term 'poem' confusing in this context and are apt to insist on making their lines rhyme. Calling the format 'a story' (see Glossary) places the writing in a more open-ended and familiar context. Children should be encouraged to use both single words and phrases in their lines and to use their word webs as sources of ideas and vocabulary.

> **G**hosts are all white
> **H**allowe'en
> **O**nly seen when it's dark
> **S**caring little children
> **T**oo spooky
> **S**aying "Ooooooohh!"

- *Engaging in fairy tale role play*

Scieszka, Jon. *The Frog Prince Continued.* Illustrated by Steve Johnson. New York: Viking Penguin, 1991.

This new look at some old fairy tales is a marvelous introduction to role-playing. In a humorous way, the author interweaves characters from a number of tales to create a larger fairy tale universe in which anything is possible.

Instead of living happily ever after, the Frog Prince runs away from a troubled relationship with the Princess and into the woods looking for a witch to turn him back into a frog. In the course of his journey he encounters, one after the other, the witches who met Sleeping Beauty, Snow White, and Hansel and Gretel. Escaping their clutches, he meets a slightly oddball version of Cinderella's Fairy Godmother, who turns him into a carriage. Fortunately, at the stroke of midnight, he turns back into a prince, realizes what a fool he's been, and returns home to his beloved princess. When they reunite, another unexpected, but entirely appropriate twist is added to the ending.

After the book has been shared and enjoyed, the teacher can brainstorm with the class a list of other evil or frightening creatures from other fairy tales or children's stories. Children will suggest characters such as the witch from ''The Wizard of Oz,'' the wolf from ''Goldilocks and the Three Bears,'' or the ogre from ''The Three Billy Goats Gruff.'' One student assumes the character of the Frog Prince and another chooses a character from the list. They then portray their version of what might happen if these two characters met.

In another extension of this activity, children can brainstorm two lists, one of 'good' characters and the other of 'evil' ones. Characters can be mixed and matched at will for role-playing. In these scenarios, Goldilocks might run into the Wicked Witch from ''The Wizard of Oz,'' or the giant from ''Jack and the Beanstalk'' might meet Sleeping Beauty. Regardless of the characters they choose, children will develop a deeper understanding of character and context through these simple and engrossing role dramas.

- *Hallowe'en storytelling*

A traditional tale called ''The Dark House,'' a children's favorite, appears in a number of picture book versions. The story gains in power and impact if the teacher can tell the tale without the prompting of a book, looking the children in the eyes and playing to their reactions.

The Dark House

In a dark, dark wood, there was a dark, dark house
And in that dark, dark house, there was a dark, dark room
And in that dark, dark room, there was a dark, dark cupboard
And in that dark, dark cupboard, there was a dark, dark shelf
And on that dark, dark shelf, there was a dark, dark, box
And in that dark, dark box, there was a GHOST!

Theme resource list

- Brown, Ruth. *A Dark Dark Tale*. London: Scholastic, 1987.

Beginning "Once upon a time there / was a dark, dark moor," this latest version of a well-loved tale uses repetitive phrasings to create a gripping, suspenseful journey to an unexpectedly charming conclusion. The sombre and hauntingly vivid drawings beautifully augment the story.

- Ciardi, John. *You Read to Me, I'll Read to You*. Illustrated by Edward Gorey. Philadelphia: J.B. Lippincott, 1962.

"What Night Would It Be?" Composed of rhyming couplets with irresistible codas for each verse, children will be 'singing' along long before the teacher can organize their choral speaking. Notice how much fun it is to say, "And a ghost cries / And the hairs rise / On the back / On the back / On the back of your neck." Moody and spooky, the poem ends by answering the title's question.

- Foster, John, ed. *A Third Poetry Book*. Oxford: Oxford University Press, 1982.

"The Blob" by Wes Magee. Breathlessly, the question "And . . . and what does it eat?" pops out. The casual answer, ". . . roast rocks and fishlegs / and x-rays and mooncrust" boggles the mind, stirs the imagination, and tickles the fancy. The ending is a perfect 'howler' for this audience.

"The Man Who Wasn't There" by Brian Lee. "Yesterday upon the stair / I met a man who wasn't there" begins this ageless and chilling description of the nameless unease and insidious fear that darkness brings to the very young (and, even the not so young). This clever metaphor puts a face on that fear and allows children to reflect on it objectively.

"Two Witches" by Alexander Resnikoff. A Hallowe'en, rhyming tongue-twister is an irresistible combination. As soon as children hear about the witch and her "itch so itchy" they'll be joining in. This short poem, only three stanzas, will get a lot of replay.

- Heidbreder, Robert. *Don't Eat Spiders*. Illustrated by Karen Patkau. Toronto: Oxford University Press, 1985.

"Here Comes the Witch." As the "bony, warty, green-faced" witch approaches, the reader is warned to stand still. This drama-filled, Hallowe'en poem is ideal as a basis for inventive enactment, for freezing into tableaux, and for teacher in role.

"Little Robot." Filled with actions and sound effects, this poem will inspire 'little robots' everywhere to rise up, stiff-armed and stiff-legged, and begin whirling around, repeating "Zoing Zoing Boink!"

• Livingston, Myra Cohn, ed. *Hallowe'en Poems.* Illustrated by Stephen Canamell. New York: Holiday Houses, 1989.

"Pumpkin, Pumpkin, Pumpkin Bright" by N.M. Bodecker. "Pumpkin, / Pumpkin, / Pumpkin bright, / When the goblins / Ride tonight" begins this clever poem patterned after the familiar "Twinkle, Twinkle, Little Star." All of the black-and-white illustrations in this collection are distinctive. On the accompanying page to this poem sits a detailed and suitably eerie jack-o'-lantern.

"Wicked Witch's Kitchen" by X.J. Kennedy. The word play and playful images create a delightfully informal and weirdly humorous effect. If you're looking for "corn on the cobweb, cauldron-hot" or "broomstick cakes and milkweed shakes," then try a visit to this witch's wonderful kitchen.

• Merriam, Eve. *Hallowe'en ABC.* Illustrated by Lane Smith. New York: Macmillan, 1987.

Each letter begins a Hallowe'en word. Some choices are gleefully 'off the wall' and refreshingly original. All are enjoyable. The letter 'u', for example, begins the word 'umbrella.' What's the connection with Hallowe'en? The verse reveals that an umbrella would be useful because "It's raining pitchforks, / it's raining cats and dogs / and loathsome toadsome / bulging bullfrogs." Eve Merriam's tasteful word play is stylishly accompanied by a set of dramatic, imaginative drawings.

• Moore, Lillian. *See My Lovely Poison Ivy.* New York: Atheneum, 1977.

"Witch Goes Shopping." This inventive, cleverly-rhyming narrative tells about a witch who goes to the local supermarket looking for such ingredients as "slugs and bugs / Snake skins dried

/ Buzzard innards" and then has to deal with her inevitable frustration.

"Teeny Tiny Ghost." Ending with "a teeny, tiny boo!" this poem is a perfect complement to the traditional, children's favorites, "Teeny, Tiny Woman" and "The Dark Night." All use repetition that builds cumulatively to a climax. A knowledge of the other poems enhances the enjoyment of the ironic ending to "Teeny Tiny Ghost."

Looking back

Some teachers choose a day close to Hallowe'en and encourage their children to come to school on that day in costume. Some schools even have the children parade in costume and award prizes in various categories. Since children in school are a captive audience, they need to be treated with sensitivity. Although the custom of dressing in costume for the purpose of 'shelling out' is a popular, traditional aspect of Hallowe'en, this activity can be problematic in the classroom. For many children, parents will supervise their participation on Hallowe'en night. Duplication at school is unnecessary. More to the point, a significant number of children are always excluded for reasons ranging from religious beliefs to parents who want to keep costumes intact for Hallowe'en night. In contrast, all children have the opportunity to celebrate the creative outcomes arising from their participation in the learning activities flowing from this unit.

Michael (age 7)

5. All about me

Children are intrigued by their own identities and the nature and condition of their immediate surroundings. They focus on such details as their own health and comfort, likes and dislikes, immediate families, homes, and relationships with their peers. The way this information is prioritized and expressed may sometimes appear arbitrary to an adult but make perfect sense to a child. The question "Who are you?" may elicit the answer "I cut my finger. We're moving tomorrow," and, with a little more prodding, "Francine." All as it should be.

   In keeping with their emergent reading and writing development in the early primary grades, children talk about and dictate stories revolving around this "All About Me" theme. With little urging and using their own mode of language, they eagerly recount their experiences with family, friends, their neighborhood, and a host of other personal topics and issues. As children tap the experiences of their own lives, the language flows. While this unit features poetry for young children, the form of the responses they make to that poetry has to be open-ended. The focus must be on relating and comparing the experiences they've had in the light of the vicarious experience of the poetry. Never fear that this kind of unit one year will 'spoil' the impact of the unit in another year. Our fascination with and attempts to define ourselves and to understand such influences as family and friends continue all our lives. Each year simply adds a few more clues to the mystery called "All About Me."

Why Can't I?

Why can't I do what I want to do
Just when I want to do it?
My bubble gum's taste
Only goes to waste
When I'm not allowed to chew it.
But "Put it away,"
My mom will say,
"And eat your dinner instead."
Well, if I can't do what I want to do,
I'd rather be sent to bed!

Why can't I say what I want to say
When a thought comes into my brain?
Later's too late
When a thought can't wait
'Cause it might not come back again.
But they always shout,
"What are you babbling about?"
They think they're really so clever.
Well, if I can't say what I want to say,
I'll never say nothin' . . . never!

Why can't I be what I want to be
Whenever I want to be it?
I can pretend I'm a car
Or fly to a star
Just 'cause I want to see it.
But, "Play with your toys
And don't make noise,"
They warn in a very stern tone.
Well, if they could be a kid like me,
I think they'd leave me alone!

Theme starter: "Why Can't I?"

In "Why Can't I?" the egocentricity of young children is explored through the child's universal battle cry, "Why can't I?" From the child's point of view, the adult world seems inexplicably arbitrary and unfair. Children empathize with the tone and mood of the narrator and with the kinds of conflict related. At the conclusion of the readaloud, children often want to discuss what has happened in each situation and relate similar experiences they've had.

Response to "Why Can't I?"

Jenny (age 7)

Follow-up suggestions for "Why Can't I?"

• Volunteers can role play, one by one, the situations presented in the three stanzas. In stanza one, for example, one child portrays the mother while another portrays the child. Discuss the premise beforehand that the child is chewing a fresh piece of gum and that it's time for dinner. Children should be encouraged to make up their own dialogue and not worry about duplicating the lines from the poem.

After discussing other courses of action or solutions to the problems apparent in the poem, volunteers can present new versions of the role play situation in which child and adult are able to resolve the conflict in a more satisfying manner.

• Children have to follow all sorts of rules set up by adults. What rules would children make up if they had the chance? Make a list on chart paper of the school rules that children suggest are fair and necessary and a brief rationale for each. Decide on the three rules that all children agree are the most important and display them in the classroom. Children can then make observing those rules a classroom goal.

Activity palette

• *Measuring 'me'*

How tall am I? How much do I weigh? These questions and others like them form the basis of an ongoing investigation into measurement and growth. Children work in pairs to complete the chart on the following page. Each pair will need a measuring tape. The classroom should also contain a personal scale for weight and a section of wall marked off beforehand in units for measuring height.

Prediction is an important element in this learning experience. For this reason, children should complete all the estimations (guesses) first. They will also need to be reassured that although these may be different from the actual measurements, guesses are never considered 'wrong'. The chart also allows children an opportunity to add measurements of their own. The results of this activity are saved, repeated three or four times during the year, and the results each time are compared to highlight the individual growth.

Measuring Me

Name: _____

Part to measure	My guess	My measurement
My weight		
Distance around my head		
Distance around my waist		
Length of my foot		
Length of my arm (from shoulder to fingertip)		
Length of my leg		

• *Creating a photomontage or collage*

For this activity, children will need scissors, glue, a large sheet of construction paper, and a variety of expendable magazines. To begin, they draw a line diagonally from one corner to another on the construction paper, separating the sheet into two equal parts. One section is labeled "All About Me Now" and the other section is labeled "All About Me Some Day."

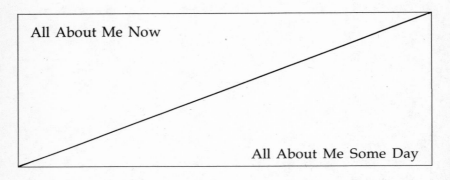

As they flip through the old magazines, the children look for and cut out items they identify with each section. "All About Me Now" will contain anything connected with themselves and their present life. "All About Me Some Day" will contain their dreams, aspirations, and an open-ended wish list. Alert the children to examine advertisements in the magazines as well as photographs and illustrations. They should also be reminded to cut out and use only those portions or items in each photo or ad that apply to them. Encourage them to overlap items for effect.

• *Writing an acrostic 'story'*

As introduced in chapter 4, "Hallowe'en and other spooky times," a word is written vertically down the left-hand margin of the paper. In this case, the word is the child's name, either just the given name or the surname as well. Each line must then start with a word beginning with the designated letter from that name. The word or phrase should have some connection with the child.

As well, an acrostic poem does not necessarily have to rhyme. Since their experience is almost entirely with rhyming poetry, children often find the term 'poem' confusing in this context and

are apt to insist on making their lines rhyme. Calling the format
'a story' (see Glossary) places the writing in a more open-ended
and familiar context.

> **F**rom London, England
> **R**eads lots of books
> **A** lot of fun to play with
> **N**ice to her friends
> **C**heerful
> **I**sn't afraid of the dark
> **N**ervous sometimes
> **E**ats apples

- *Making lists*

When adults get acquainted, they inevitably offer and compare
basic information about themselves, including likes, dislikes, and
personal preferences. Children do the same. In a preliminary
and concrete way, this kind of data exchange helps identify and
distinguish who we are both for ourselves and for others. With
the familiarity and understanding built on this foundation, a discussion of values and beliefs can develop.

The following chart, *Getting to Know Me*, can be combined with
the plasticine portrait, page 55, to create a personal profile
display.

All about me

Ian (age 7)

Getting to Know Me

Name: _____

Birthdate: _____

Foods I like to eat: _____

_____

_____

Games I like to play: _____

_____

_____

_____

Programs I like to watch on television: _____

_____

_____

_____

Things that make me happy: _____

_____

_____

_____

Some other things I like: _____

_____

_____

_____

Something else about me I'd like to tell: _____

_____

_____

_____

- *Sculpting self-portraits from plasticine*
Reid, Barbara. *Playing with Plasticine*. Toronto: Kids Can Press, 1988.

In the chapter entitled *For Keeps* children are shown how to create self-portraits from plasticine as well as portraits of family and friends. Starting with instructions on how to use cardboard as a surface that can be later hung or left standing free, the artist directs children to a mirror and photos to observe specific characteristics. The picture is slowly built up from outline shape to facial features to hair. With Reid's own self-portrait on the back cover as inspiration, children will thoroughly enjoy adding to their own portrait gallery. For a full description of the contents and organization of Barbara Reid's book, see chapter 3, "Animals, animals, everywhere."

- *Investigating through research*
Farris, Katherine. *I Didn't Know That!* Toronto: Greey de Pencier Books, 1988.

With accompanying full-color photographs and illustrations, children's questions about themselves, their bodies, and their world are listed, one after another. Here are a few samples from the hundreds included in this soft-cover volume:

Why does sunshine make you feel good?
What makes your stomach growl?
Why do you get a headache when you eat ice cream too fast?

The answers are fascinating and concise.

Theme resource list

- Bober, Natalie S., ed. *Let's Pretend*. Illustrated by Bill Bell. New York: Viking Kestrel, 1986.

"Changing" by Mary Ann Hoberman. To be a child means to be egocentric. As children grow older, they gradually become more aware of another person's perspective. In this poem children are gently invited to consider "What fun it would be / if I could try you out / and you could try me."

"Every Time I Climb a Tree" by David McCord. A child's perspective can never be quite the same after the first time he or she climbs up high, looks down, and then looks beyond. The scrapes and scares incurred in getting there are worth it when ''. . . I am free / Every time I climb a tree.''

• Bodecker, N.M. *Snowman Sniffles*. New York: A Margaret K. McElderry Book, 1983.

''I'm Never as Good as I Want to Be.'' This simple but penetrating poem begins, ''I'm never as good as I want to be, / and sometimes too bad when I'm bad.'' The poem gently exposes the issue of children's self-esteem and the kind of adult arrogance that sometimes brings that self-esteem into question.

• Foster, John, ed. *A First Poetry Book*. New York: Oxford University Press, 1985.

''The Mystery Creatures'' by Wes Magee. Who are these strange creatures who ''dig food from dirt,'' while the ''young squeal like pigs if you / tickle their feet''? Children will delight in seeing themselves and their world through alien eyes. The utterly novel perspective is illuminating.

''This Is the Hand'' by Michael Rosen. Patterned loosely on the structure of ''This Is the House that Jack Built,'' this light-hearted verse explores the wondrous curiosity of childhood. The central motif follows a child's hand through a variety of experiences, for example, sliding ''. . . round the bath / to find the soap / that wouldn't float.'' The cumulative, final verse neatly recaps all the experiences.

• Merriam, Eve. *Blackberry Ink*. Illustrated by Hans Wilhelm. New York: William Morrow, 1985.

''Something's in My Pocket.'' What treasures might you find in a child's pocket? This tongue-in-cheek recital of possibilities decides, among many others, that ''It isn't a cookie / That's nice and stale.''

• Prelutsky, Jack, ed. *The Random House Book of Poetry for Children*. Illustrated by Arnold Hobel. New York: Random House, 1983.

''Just Me'' by Margaret Hillert. ''Nobody sees what I can see, / For back of my eyes there is only me.'' Everyone is unique and special. "Just Me" celebrates the individual and encourages children to accept the fact that they are just right for who they are — themselves.

- Rosen, Michael. *Freckly Feet and Itchy Knees.* Illustrated by Sami Sweeten. London: William Collin's Sons, 1990.

When Michael Rosen announces, "I'm talking about noses," he unveils a riotous discussion of assorted body parts — hands, feet, eyes, knees, bellies, and the places and situations in which they're found. This gleeful book is filled with spontaneous repetition and playful illustrations. The ending is an uproarious, glorious culmination of sound effects.

- Silverstein, Shel. *Where the Sidewalk Ends.* New York: Harper and Row, 1974.

"Hug o' War." The message 'make love not war' adapted for the world of children becomes "I will not play at tug o' war / I'd rather play at hug o' war." The values in this poem are laudable, the tone is upbeat and positive, and the message is worth spreading.

"Listen to the Mustn'ts." After detailing the mustn'ts, don'ts, shouldn'ts, won'ts, and all the rest of the negative messages children hear, Silverstein turns the whole perspective completely around and opens up the world of the possible. With self-esteem such a crucial issue, children need to hear someone say, "Anything can happen, child, / anything can be."

- Simmie, Lois. *An Armadillo Is Not a Pillow.* Illustrations by Anne Simmie. Saskatchewan: Western Producer Prairie Books, 1986.

"Playhouse" identifies a child's need for a safe, secret place and knowingly itemizes all the benefits of a childhood sanctum sanctorum. In part, a playhouse is "A place for wishing, a place for dreaming."

Looking back

Although the activities in this unit focus on the theme "All About Me," they can easily be adapted to help children learn about others. As the lists, stories, drawings, and other creations springing from the unit begin to mount up in the classroom, they can be used for personal research. Children can be invited to explore the classroom displays in search of specific kinds of information. They can look for someone who shares a similar interest, pet, or aspiration, they can discover some facet of another individual they hadn't known before, or they can identify an item they admire that someone else has created. In the discussions that follow this research, the children's talk will be full of other people and their accomplishments and, as they share what they've learned about others, everyone's perspective and awareness will grow.

Response to "Why Can't I?"

Jeffrey (age 7)

6. In the city

Relatively little poetry about life in the city has been written for children. Traditionally, rural settings and imagery rooted in the natural world have dominated poetry written about people's daily environment. Since, in adult literature, urban and rural values have been represented as antithetical, it's not surprising that this same conflict surfaces in children's literature, as in the tale "The City Mouse and the Country Mouse." For children who have never known any other environment except the city, poems that describe a peaceful, sylvan life they've never known or that decry a crowded, polluted atmosphere over which they have no control tell only part of the story.

Fortunately, in the attempt to recreate experience through a child's sensibilities, many contemporary poets writing for children have come to realize how life in a city is seen through the eyes of a child. Wonder, inspiration, and exhilaration can also be found in a sandlot playground, a towering skyscraper, or the hungry jaws of a backhoe. The poetry that follows is a balanced collection. While some of the poems celebrate the wonders of the city, others describe the difficult integration of the natural and human worlds, and some point to the serious, problematic issues that city life presents. Whatever the focus, children need reassurance that where they live has no bearing on who they are or the values they represent. In the world of poetry, where you look for truth doesn't matter. How you look does.

Theme starter: "Sounds of the City"

In the following poem, the relentless rhythm and repetition in

Sounds of the City

Early-morning traffic tries to creep downtown
Concrete mixer rolls around and around
Taxicab horn makes a hard, harsh sound
Subway rumbling underground, underground

While towers of glass gleam sunshine bright
Far above the noises in a silent light
Towers of steel where the high winds blow
Echo with the grinding of the traffic below

Garbage-can lid lying on the street
Tap it with a stick for the beat, beat, beat
Skipping rope slapping under prancing feet
Skateboard rattling on the rough concrete

While towers of glass gleam sunshine bright
Bathing the children in a golden light
Towers of steel where the high winds blow
Echo with the laughter of the children below

the rhyme scheme, as well as the content of the first two verses, set up a tension that represents the stereotypical beginning to another day in the big city. In contrast, the sounds of children at play change the tone of the poem and the way in which we view the city, to the extent that the towers in the last stanza have been transformed into benign, protective images. Before the readaloud, teachers may suggest that children listen for specific sounds and pictures in the poem.

Follow-up suggestions for "Sounds of the City"

• Choral reading can be enhanced with sound effects. In this case, however, a little goes a long way. Too many effects simply overwhelm the language of the poem. For the first two verses, some engine sounds interspersed with horn honks give the impression of a traffic jam in the background. For the last two verses, these sounds drop away and are replaced by the regular tapping, finger snapping, and hand clapping suggested by children at play. The volunteers who supply the sound effects tend to approach the task in a literal manner. Since the sounds of a subway rumbling or a skateboard clattering are difficult to represent, an impressionistic approach will produce satisfying results.

• The content in this poem lends itself to depiction in mural form. A group of interested children can discuss what elements should be included in the mural and make a list of the suggestions. They should also be encouraged to augment the poem's content with their own ideas. After deciding what medium to work in, they can divide the tasks and begin to sketch the scene. A copy of the poem can be displayed along with the finished mural.

Activity palette

• *Constructing a three-dimensional city*
Using the suggestions found in the following resource book, children can construct their own city out of scrap materials.

Grater, Michael. *Fun Models*. London: Macdonald, 1987.

This simple step-by-step guide to making models begins by encouraging children to collect scrap materials, mostly cardboard and plastic. A number of suggestions are then offered for cutting out shapes, making them stand, and decorating them. Specific instructions for making rooves, trains, wheeled vehicles, and even tractors prepare children for constructing their own, three-dimensional city, complete with vehicles and inhabitants. This 'hands-on' response allows children to concretely visualize, adapt, and experiment with some of the concepts involved in city life.

In the city

Dwayne (age 7)

• *Building with manipulative materials*

Most primary classrooms contain creative, manipulative materials such as Lego or Tinker Toys. One challenge during this unit could be to create a building distinctive to a particular city out of those materials. A city's skyline usually has a few distinguishing features, such as a sports stadium, a city hall, a suspension bridge, or a tall or uniquely-shaped office building. Other challenges might be to construct a type of vehicle found in the city or different types of dwelling places.

• *Comparing and categorizing characteristics*

On chart paper or an overhead transparency, the teacher places the title "In the city." During a brainstorming session, suggestions from the children about what they would expect to find in that environment are listed. Afterwards, the same procedure is followed for "In the country." During brainstorming, all suggestions are accepted and listed without comment or discussion. After the brainstorming, two columns entitled "In the city" and "In the country" are headed up side by side on chart paper. The children then choose items from the original brainstorming sheets that match up and can now be placed together for comparison.

In the city	*In the country*
lots of cars	not much traffic
tall buildings	barns or silos
sidewalks	trees and fields

In a final step, children can try to group and categorize the items in any way that seems to make sense. Characteristics then might be subheaded "What people do," "Things people use," or "How the outside looks."

• *Painting seasonal city pictures*

In many activity-based primary classrooms, at least part of the day is spent at learning centres. During a unit on the city, children can be challenged at the painting centre to represent the change of seasons in the city. They first need to choose a single, outside location. For children who live in a city, an actual location, such as a playground or the street outside their home, is best. They then paint separate pictures of that setting in spring, summer, fall, and winter. Lined up side by side, the pictures stimulate valuable comparison and discussion.

Theme resource list

- Bober, Natalie S., ed. *Let's Pretend*. Illustrated by Bill Bell. New York: Viking Kestrel, 1986.

"Snowy Morning" by Lilian Moore. Phrased in deceptively simple language and imbued with an insistent, flowing rhythm and an intricate rhyme, "Snowy Morning" dramatically captures the moment when a city is magically transformed by the first snowfall. City dwellers will instantly recognize and relive that surreal instant when "no brake growls, / no siren howls and / no horns / blow."

- Foster, John, ed. *A First Poetry Book*. New York: Oxford University Press, 1985.

"Building Site" by Marian Lines. A rain-drenched housing project is the context for this mouth-filling, highly inventive, sensory exploration. As we become acquainted with the "Drowned, brown, rain-washed plain. / Straining cranes, / Bucking trucks," the internal rhymes and onomatopoeic images set up echoes and tensions that intermingle with the theme.

"Carbreakers" by Marian Lines. Where do cars go when they die? This poem answers that question with metaphor-rich verses about a car graveyard. As the last verse concludes at night with ". . . a sound / Of ghostly horns that moan and whine," the ending seems eerily inevitable, fitting, and resonant.

"House" by Leonard Clark. In this moody, evocative poem, an old house sits in ruins: "Locks are broken, every wall / Looks as if about to fall." The poignant ending recalls happier times and gently touches on the bittersweet nature of time and reality.

"There's a Red Brick Wall" by Nancy Chambers. Anyone who's lived in a city in the height of summer can identify with the experience of walking by a red brick wall "that stands and burns / in the sun's hot heat." Just two stanzas, the poem glows with the heat and the symbiotic relationship of people and their surroundings.

• Hall, Donald, ed. *The Oxford Book of Children's Verse in America*. New York: Oxford University Press, 1985.

"August" by John Updike. What happens in August when "The sprinkler twirls / The summer wanes. / The pavement wears / Popsicle stains"? In exact, concise images, this deceptively simple poem describes how people escape the summer doldrums by going to the beach. Children particularly delight in the last two lines.

• Hopkins, Lee Bennett, ed. *A Song in Stone, City Poems*. New York: Thomas Y. Crowell, 1983.

"The City Dump" by Felice Holtman. In a tumbling tangle of color and rhyme, the refuse of a city dump is transformed into a curiously compelling feast for the scavengers and the poet's eye alike — "a carnival / on the garbage heap."

"Manhattan Lullabye" by Norma Tarber. Little poetry is written for city children about city children. Traffic and concrete have a way of discouraging rhyme. "Manhattan Lullabye" takes the sounds of the city and lets "these city girls and boys / dream a music in the noise."

"Sidewalk Measles" by Barbara M. Hales. In this extended metaphor, the poet sees "the sidewalk catch the measles" as the rain comes down. The rhymes are full, harsh, and fitting and the images are sharp, inventive, and vivid.

• Merriam, Eve. *A Word or Two with You*. New York: Atheneum, 1981.

"Frying Pan in the Moving Van." The premise for this cumulative poem is simple. When a new family moves into the house next door, the narrator describes the contents of the moving van. As the teller adds detail after detail, the chorus keeps demanding, "What did you see? / Tell, tell, tell." Take a deep, deep breath before trying the last-verse recapitulation. "Frying Pan in the Moving Van" is a perfect vehicle for some fun-filled choral speaking.

• Merriam, Eve. *Blackberry Ink*. Illustrated by Hans Wilhelm. New York: William Morrow, 1985.

"It Fell in the City." Whatever "fell" in the city is never

identified, but colors of the city, from "black rooftops" to "green garbage cans," all turn white.

• Prelutsky, Jack, ed. *The Random House Book of Poetry for Children*. Illustrated by Arnold Hobel. New York: Random House, 1983.

"City, City" by Marci Ridlon. The ambivalence people feel about city life is cleverly captured in this two-part poem. While the first section begins "City, city, / Wrong and bad, / Looms above me / When I'm sad," the second section starts on a brighter note when the narrator is glad. The form of this long, thin poem imitates a tall skyscraper. The unique characteristics that make city life so exciting and frustrating tumble out in apt and rapid rhymes.

"Sing a Song of People" by Lois Lenski. One of the predominant characteristics of any city is the constant parade of impersonal, idiosyncratic strangers. This poem celebrates city people in all their diversity.

Looking back

A unit on life in the city inevitably leads to a discussion of pollution. Rather than deal with the second-hand complaints and opinions children have garnered from adults, many teachers prefer a direct, experiential approach to the issue. The adult world contains problems that children have difficulty understanding and over which they have no control. In their own school and home environment, those same issues take on a concrete form. Outfitted with gloves and plastic bags, for example, children can investigate the litter in the schoolyard. After discovering what it is, how much there is, and where it came from, they can then decide what they personally can do to publicize and alleviate the problem. After dealing with recycling and the elimination of waste in the classroom environment, children can take a similar, proactive stance at home. The values children develop as they work through and solve such problems on a small scale will hold them in good stead when they join the adult world.

7. The world outside

A child's first step beyond the front door is important. The inside world is secure and predictible, extensively explored on hands and knees and known in intricate detail. The world outside is entirely different, vast and unpredictable and filled with risks needing to be taken. Whether it's the discovery of rain or an earthworm, the investigation follows the same course. Children want to know what it's called, what it does, and how it affects them. On the other hand, you can tell them more than they want to know. What children want to know is directly related to the kind of tangible, experientially-based, and egocentric way they encounter the world. The story about the young child coming home and asking his parent where he came from is a case in point. After the parent delivers the dreaded and awkward lecture on the facts of life, of course, the child says, ''That's fine, but Bobby said he was from Chicago and I wanted to know where I came from.''

For this reason, children need to direct their own learning. Through independent investigation, they construct their own version of reality. They pose questions, find answers, and then test those answers. As they change their questions, they also change the kind of answers they receive, and the kind of reality they see. With individual development over time and a rich variety of experience, children develop a certain objectivity and, at some point, are ready for the next stage of questioning. As we try to make sense of our world and, in the process, ourselves, the questions never stop. As adults, we continue to question and to learn. The poems that follow offer children a tapestry of unique, vicarious experiences. The vivid, compelling scenes and

The World Outside

The world outside is hard to know,
How worms can see or rainbows glow,
Why my tongue's smooth and a cat's is rough,
Or how much chocolate cake's enough.

Why schools have tests you have to pass,
What makes the milk when cows eat grass,
Why moths aren't known as 'flutterbies',
Or what makes tears when someone cries.

Why nightmares only come at night,
Why caterpillars never fight,
How planes can fly or yo-yos spin,
Or why people have different colored skin.

Or what makes flowers grow,
Or why the wind begins to blow.

The outside world is very hard to know.

enlightening perspectives will provide more answers and stimulate more questions.

Theme starter: "The World Outside"

"The World Outside" is filled with questions. When children first hear this poem, their initial reaction is often to ask or answer the questions that directly interest them. While some of the questions clearly are from an adult's perspective as focussed through a child's eyes, others seem more genuinely child-like and these observations are the ones that first catch children's attention. To capitalize on the format of the poem, teachers often suggest that children listen for questions they would like to have answered or to which they already know the answers.

Follow-up suggestions for "The World Outside"

• Initially, the discussion after the readaloud should revolve around those questions from the poem that children find most intriguing. The teacher might consider recording these questions on chart paper, leaving a space below each one for an answer. Some answers can be immediately derived from children's direct background knowledge and filled in on the chart. The rest of the questions can be re-examined at regular intervals or as individual children research those areas.
• Since the poem is made up of individual questions arbitrarily organized, that feature can be emphasized during choral reading. The first line and the last three lines are read by the group. Volunteers then pick a line to read aloud by themselves. When interpreted in this manner, the questions pop out from all over the class and are framed by the more sedately-paced and reflective common elements.

Activity palette

• *Creating a learning centre (the finding-out place)*
The core of this unit is personal investigation, children asking and answering questions about the nature of their world. A learning centre in the classroom specifically devoted to this kind of investigation can facilitate individual learning not just for the duration of this unit but on an ongoing basis. This 'finding-out

place' could be located on a small table or it could be comprised of two desks placed together. In anticipation of the wide spectrum of research needs, the learning centre should contain as many learning tools and reference books as possible. A selection could be made from such items as the following:

- magnifying glass   — microscope
- balance scale   — measuring tape
- aquarium   — terrarium
- shells   — rocks
- plants   — atlas
- reference books (animals, insects, rocks and minerals, weather, astronomy)
- filmstrip viewer (a variety of filmstrips)

If learning centres are an integral component of the classroom program, a 'finding-out place' can be integrated into the normal routine. If not, the resources can be utilized whenever an individual or a group display a need to investigate a particular issue or area of study. As questions develop from large-group discussions, individuals can be designated to investigate or research on the group's behalf and to report back. Questions needn't be answered immediately. Throughout the day, as questions arise spontaneously, they can be placed on flashcards and displayed at the centre.

How do our goldfish breathe?

What happens to worms in the winter?

After a successful investigation, the answer can be displayed at the 'finding-out place' along with the question.

- *Sculpting pictures with plasticine*
Reid, Barbara. *Playing with Plasticine*. Toronto: Kids Can Press, 1988.

In the chapter entitled "Paint a Picture," the author shows children how to use the full potential of plasticine to develop total pictures with background, foreground, and texture. Skyscapes, landscapes, garden scenes, and the far reaches of space are just some of the possibilities explored. Since 'experiments' can easily be repaired or changed, children are encouraged to take risks with this medium. For a full description of the contents and organization of Barbara Reid's book, see page 31.

- *Making mobiles of the outside world*
Grater, Michael. *Fun Movers*. London: Macdonald, 1987.

In quick order, this simple but effective, step-by-step guide to making mobiles sets the stage for children to begin responding to the natural world. Possibilities for shape, color, pattern, material, techniques for hanging, and three-dimensional effects are described in print and through illustrations. Children can develop their own mobiles with nature themes such as fish, birds, insects, flowers, leaves, waves, clouds, or whatever else stirs their interests and imaginations. The characteristic movement of the mobiles will add further enjoyment and stimulation when the creations are displayed in the classroom.

- *Exploring the neighborhood*
With this kind of theme, taking the class outside becomes essential. Short walking tours provide invaluable experiences to help children understand their immediate surroundings and to stimulate investigation. A walk around the school and nearby streets offers the opportunity to create maps of the area. A simple visit to a playground or a park leads to direct observations of plants, birds, insects, clouds, and the effects of a particular season on the environment. Discussions, picture-making, writing, and reading are just a few of the activities stimulated by such informal field trips.

Theme resource list

- Bauer, Caroline Feller, ed. *Snowy Day Stories and Poems*. New York: J.B. Lippincott, 1986.

"Snow" by Mary Ann Hoberman. "Snow" includes pleasing repetition, an irresistible, chanting rhythm, and vivid, concrete images. "Snow in the sandbox / Snow on the slide / Snow on the bicycle / Left outside." By the second reading, children will spontaneously join in.

Bober, Natalie, S., ed. *Let's Pretend*. Illustrated by Bill Bell. New York: Viking Kestrel, 1986.

"Souvenir" by David McCord. In a series of evocative, rhyming couplets, the palpable, detailed characteristics of an ocean-shore experience tumble out, after the narrator says, "I bring back a shell so I can always hear / the music of the ocean when I hold it to my ear."

"The Night Will Never Stay" by Eleanor Farjeon. In just a few, simple lines, this wistful, gentle favorite touches the imagination and moves the heart. The compelling, crystal images culminate in the ambivalent reminder that "the night will slip away / like sorrow or a tune."

• Bodecker, N.M. *Snowman Sniffles*. New York: A Margaret K. McElderry Book, 1983.

"At winter's end / a snowman grows / a snowdrop / on his carrot nose." Witty, insightful, thought-provoking images dot these luscious verses. As winter 'sniffs' into spring, children will want this charming poem read again and again.

• Cole, Joanna, ed. *A New Treasury of Children's Poetry*. New York: Doubleday and Company, 1984.

"Fireworks" by Valerie Worth. The form of this poem aptly suits the theme. Beginning "First / A far thud, / Then the rocket / Climbs the air, / A dull red flare," the poem builds from the single projectile to the glorious shower of colorful images exploding at the end. Children leap at the chance to respond graphically, either individually or in pairs, with their own fireworks displays. Oil pastels or crayons on black construction paper create a startling and satisfying effect.

"Galoshes" by Rhoda Bacmeister. Language and experience are intrinsically joined in this exuberant romp through slush and mud. The unabashed use of alliteration and deliberate rhythms make rhyme unnecessary. The sheer joy of saying, "Susie's galoshes / Make splishes and sploshes" vicariously duplicates the exultant act itself.

"Sunflakes" by Frank Asch. This simple but brilliant transposition suggests that "If sunlight fell like snowflakes, . . . we could build a sunman." The hypothetical situations that follow this opening are inventive and intriguing. The last line leads naturally to all the other questions, answers, and further images that a young audience will be so glad to supply.

• Foster, John, ed. *A First Poetry Book*. New York: Oxford University Press, 1985.

"The Spinning Earth" by Aileen Fisher. If you've never questioned whether or not the earth actually spins, you probably haven't looked closely around you. How can you really tell when "houses don't go whirling by, / or puppies swirl around the sky"? A child's right to reserved skepticism, even in the face of adult authority, is perfectly captured in the wondering, whimsical tone.

"Winter Morning" by Ogden Nash. As well as the inventive word play and the wry perspective you would expect to find in an Ogden Nash poem, "Winter Morning" also presents a number of delicious word pictures as winter begins turning "houses into birthday cakes."

• Foster, John, ed. *A Third Poetry Book*. Oxford: Oxford University Press, 1982.

"Snowflakes" by Clive Sanson. In this poem, an entire science lesson unfolds delicately, lovingly, and with a genuine sense of wonder. Although the focus seems to be on the wonders of snowflakes, as images develop, we discover that snowflakes can assume many forms.

• Hall, Donald, ed. *The Oxford Book of Children's Verse in America*. New York: Oxford University Press, 1985.

"April Rain Song" by Langston Hughes. Although "April Rain Song" doesn't rhyme, it does sing with the gloriously vibrant language of Langston Hughes. From the invitational opening, "Let the rain kiss you," to the emotional sense of wonder in the closing phrase, the images shimmer with inner beauty, immediacy, and a gentle, open clarity.

• Martin Jr., Bill and John Archambault. *Listen to the Rain.* Illustrated by James Endicott. New York: Henry Holt, 1988.

This picture book displays a delicate, sensitive use of natural language, full of alliterative, internal rhymes and echoic, evocative imagery culminating in "the fresh / wet / silent / after-time / of rain."

• Prelutsky, Jack, ed. *The Random House Book of Poetry for Children.* Illustrated by Arnold Hobel. New York: Random House, 1983.

"Hey, Bug!" by Lilian Moore. As we grow older (and taller), we get further (and farther) from the fascinating world of insects. From the excited, opening shout of "Hey, bug, stay! / Don't run away," this poem recreates the quality of up-close investigation and sense of kinship children spontaneously feel for all manner of living things.

"The Muddy Puddle" by Dennis Lee. As the young narrator, fully clothed, slowly settles into the mud puddle, children happily exult in the vivid sensations and the delicious language.

Looking back

The core of these investigations into the outside world has been independent 'problem-finding.' Many of the activities have led children to pose questions about issues that intrigue them and then collaboratively discover the answers. When they discover that they can personally control the course of their learning through the questions they ask, children effectively take over responsibility for their own learning. This kind of approach can enrich any unit and any theme. To make the approach work, teachers need to strike a balance between the planning and structure necessary to ensure a depth of content to meet children's needs and the flexibility required to allow children to access and shape that content in individual ways. Without structure, the unit flounders; without flexibility, learning is impeded.

8. Imaginings

The kinds of books that are written for children are based on fairy tales, peopled with anthropomorphic animals, or wildly fantastic in imitation of the rich, make-believe life of childhood. For this reason, children come to equate imagination with originality and make-believe, something inspired that appears out of nowhere. Those who can come up with these ideas are 'creative' and those who can't are left to wonder about the gift they lack and what they have to do to get it. Is it any wonder, then, that imagination is often misunderstood?

Professional writers, of course, know very well that imaginative fiction is clearly rooted in the real world. Speculative fiction, often called science fiction or science fantasy, is a case in point. These flights of fancy actually stem from observations made about the present. Science fiction authors tend to ask themselves what would happen if one or more variables in the present were changed. They project the altered present into the future and examine the outcome. Everyone can and should wonder "what if" from time to time.

The exercise is both instructive and fun. In the unit that follows, children are given concrete models and specific direction to help them find their own pathway into the world of imaginings.

Theme Starter: "What If?"

This poem illustrates the main ingredient in the process of imagining. One variable in a number of real situations is altered and the effect of that alteration is predicted. Children respond enthusiastically to the feeling that anything is possible.

What If?

What if roads were made of rubber,
Would cars bounce around the block?
And if turtles went to college,
Would they soon learn how to talk?

What if worms wore plastic sneakers,
Would they wear them to a dance?
And if chickens wore suspenders,
Would they lay eggs dressed in pants?

What if clouds were chocolate ice cream,
And what if rain was soda pop,
Would children then love rainy days
And wish they'd never stop?

Follow-up suggestions for "What If?"

• Children love to invent their own 'what ifs'. A useful preliminary to this activity can be handled in a large-group situation. The teacher selects a concrete object from the classroom, such as a chair, and asks for ways in which it could be changed. Children might suggest that it be made of balloons or paper or rubber, or that it have enormously long legs or be put together with hinges. For each characteristic, the teacher asks what effect that might have. The key, at this stage, is to take as many suggestions as possible to reinforce the idea that there is no one 'right' answer. Then another object can be chosen and the process repeated. When the frame of reference is broadened to include the world outside the classroom, the children are ready to start speculating on their own.

• Children also love to illustrate 'what ifs'. They should feel free to choose a favorite image from the poem or to use one of their own or one developed by a classmate. To ensure that it makes sense next day or to an outside observer, the illustration can be captioned with the printed speculation that led to the drawing. "What would happen if chairs were made of balloons?" might accompany a drawing of a chair and its occupant floating off into the sky.

Activity palette

• *Storytelling through wordless books*

Wordless books offer a marvelous route into the wonders of reading and storytelling. As children examine and explain the graphic elements, they are making sense of the story in a way that directly parallels the reading of print. Since these books contain little, if any, print, children can tell or 'read' the story in their own language and mode of expression. Wordless books teach children what reading is all about and how to take control of their own reading processes. They are also fascinating doors into the world of the imagination. A few samples follow.

Van Allsburg, Chris. *Ben's Dream*. Boston: Houghton Mifflin, 1982.

Framed at beginning and end by text that can be read aloud by

Response to "What If?"

Crystal (age 7)

Jenny (age 7)

the teacher, the rest of Ben's dream unfolds in evocative, black-and-white sketches. On a rainy day, a boy falls asleep while reading a geography book about the world's famous landmarks. In his dream, his tiny house floats on a huge sea past the Sphinx, the leaning tower of Pisa, and many more celebrated scenes. He also sees his sister. When he awakes, the question arises as to whether or not he was actually dreaming.

Wiesner, David. *Free Fall*. New York: Lothrop, Lee, and Sheppard Books, 1988.

A boy falls asleep while reading. In his dream, elements of his room — his bed cover, chess set, the book he was reading, and his goldfish — are transformed and transported into a parallel universe full of adventure and a strange, puzzling journey. The illustrations are intricate, rich in detail, fluidly drawn, and wistfully shaded in muted tones.

Wiesner, David. *Tuesday*. New York: Clarion Books, 1991.

Tuesday evening, around eight, countless frogs atop flying lily pads arise from their swamp and head for town. Although no people see them, they spend the evening creating havoc wherever they go. Come morning, they drop from the sky and head back to the swamp, leaving their lily pads behind to befuddle the local police. The book ends on the following Tuesday evening when we realize that if frogs can fly so can pigs!

• *Writing in a variety of genres*

Ahlberg, Janet and Allan Ahlberg. *The Jolly Postman or Other People's Letters*. London: William Heinemann; Boston: Little, Brown, 1986.

Using well-known fairy tales and their characters as springboards, the Ahlbergs interweave entertainment with models featuring an unusually rich and varied kaleidoscope of purposeful writing. Through these models, children have unique opportunities to review events through another's eyes and to witness and experience a wide range of written genres. The models also offer an open-ended framework for engaging in further role play, writing-in-role, writing for specific audiences, and reinterpreting well-known tales.

   After sharing the picture book with their classes, teachers can assist with brainstorming lists of possible spinoff activities. A list of other fairy tales and their main characters not used in the book can yield numerous possibilities. Each fairy tale can be matched with suggestions for sender and receiver, purpose, and type of writing. When completed, these communications can be placed in addressed envelopes, roles assigned for individuals to receive the letters, the letters delivered by a 'postman', and then shared. At this point, further activities will grow spontaneously.

• *Imaginings in water*

To direct activities at the water table, ask the children to imagine what it would be like if people lived in the oceans instead of on land. What if our planet were totally covered in water? After a group has had an opportunity to role play at the water table, they can debrief with the teacher and discuss their impressions, discoveries, and questions.

• *Imaginings in sand*

The adult science fiction classic *Dune* featured a planet of sand as its major setting. To direct activities at the sand table, ask the children to imagine what it would be like to live on a planet totally made of sand. After a group has had an opportunity to role play at the sand table, they can debrief with the teacher and discuss their impressions, discoveries, and questions.

Theme resource list

• Ahlberg, Janet and Allan Ahlberg. *The Jolly Postman or Other People's Letters.* London: William Heinemann; Boston: Little, Brown, 1986.

"Once upon a bicycle, / So they say, / A Jolly Postman came one day / From over the hills / And far away. . . ." So begins a gloriously wry and witty book in which the form and the content are perfectly matched. The Postman's first stop is the cottage of the Three Bears. The next page in the book is actually an envelope, suitably addressed. The envelope opens to reveal a letter from Goldilocks in which she states, in part, "I am very sory indeed that I cam into your house and ate Baby Bears Porij." In similar fashion, beginning with an illustration and a short poem, the various stops on the Postman's route are revealed one by one. A witch's catalogue arrives at the 'Gingerbread Bungalow', a postcard from Jack arrives for 'Mr. V. Bigg', a publisher asks Cinderella's permission to print her story (a sample copy is enclosed, of course), the lawyer for Miss Riding-Hood and the Three Little Pigs serves notice to 'B.B. Wolf, Esq.,'' and a birthday card is delivered to Goldilocks. (See *Activity palette*, page 78, for follow-up activities.)

• Cole, Joanna, ed. *A New Treasury of Children's Poetry*. New York: Doubleday, 1984.

''I Can Fly'' by Felice Holman. Being contained in a metal airplane is one kind of flying experience. Flying with the spontaneous freedom of a bird is another. At some point, we've all wondered what it would be like to fly. In this poem, the narrator casually says, ''I spread my arms / Like wings, / Lean on the wind, / And my body zings / About.'' Enjoyable in its own right, ''I Can Fly'' can also stimulate discussion and investigation of a variety of 'what if' situations.

''There Once Was a Puffin'' by Florence Page Jaques. Six stanzas tell the charming story of how the lonely little puffin came to stop feasting on little fishes and to start playing with them. Children appreciate and easily relate to the understated moral.

''Wynken, Blynken, and Nod'' by Eugene Field casts a timeless spell. In spite of the traditional images, predictable rhymes, and sing-song rhythms, or, perhaps, because of them, the wonder of youthful imagination remains fresh and genuinely touching. As with so many memorable tales, just the familiar opening lines, ''Wynken, Blynken, and Nod one night / Sailed off in a wooden shoe, / Sailed in a river of crystal light / Into a sea of dew,'' are enough to set the stage and establish the mood for a unique and wistful, lyrical journey.

• Foster, John, ed. *A Third Poetry Book*. Oxford: Oxford University Press, 1982.

''Lizzie and the Apple Tree'' by Julie Holder. What would happen if you climbed into an apple tree and refused to come down? In this unusual story poem, a young girl named Lizzie ''swung her legs / and laughed at their frown.'' Children enjoy blurting out the bizarre and somewhat predictable ending.

• Gay, Marie-Louise. *Rainy Day Magic*. Toronto: Stoddart, 1987.

After exhausting all their usual pastimes while playing inside on a rainy day, two young friends stumble into wild adventures in a world of imagination. The transition is made quickly as "The blue turned to purple / Then black and then gray." The riotous escapades that follow in this picture book are cleverly scripted and inventively illustrated.

- Hall, Donald, ed. *The Oxford Book of Children's Verse in America*. New York: Oxford University Press, 1985.

"Adventures of Isabel" by Ogden Nash. If you're looking for a strong female protagonist, meet Isabel. When threatened by an enormous bear, "Isabel, Isabel, didn't worry, / Isabel didn't scream or scurry." A wicked witch, a hideous giant, and a "troublesome doctor" are, in turn, handled in emphatic and unusual ways. (In some recent collections, the verse featuring the doctor has been expunged. This anthology contains all the original verses.) The rhymes are delightful and the situations are clever and inventive. This favorite can be read and enjoyed over and over.

"Books Fall Open" by David McCord. One message needs to be conveyed to and modeled for children over and over again. When David McCord begins "Books fall open, / you fall in, / delighted where / you've never been," he reveals the true power and potential of the written word. Although a line or two might be too elaborately phrased, on the whole, the poem glows with wisdom, clarity, and truth.

"The Tale of Custard the Dragon" by Ogden Nash. This long, narrative poem begins simply and calmly, informing us that "Belinda lived in a little, white house." After that opening, however, the poem turns into a flight into the fantastic, a "realio, trulio, little pet dragon" notwithstanding. Children empathize with the cowardly dragon named Custard, thrill to the invasion of a pirate through the window, and celebrate Custard's brief but satisfying triumph. The rhymes are riotous, the rhythm bubbles along, and the story is exquisite. Children remember this poem and request it years after their first encounter.

Prelutsky, Jack, ed. *The Random House Book of Poetry for Children*. Illustrated by Arnold Hobel. New York: Random House, 1983.

"To Dark Eyes Dreaming" by Zilpha Keatley Snyden. All about dreams, this poem rhymes in unpredictable, internal patterns. The special rhyme scheme and the arrangement of phrases and sentences on the lines moulds the form to the theme. The last few lines hauntingly conclude that dreams "will not fly except in open sky. / A fenced-in dream / will die."

• Silverstein, Shel. *Where the Sidewalk Ends.* New York: Harper and Row, 1974.

"Jimmy Jet and his TV Set." How harmful to young children is watching too much television? Only Shel Silverstein could take this controversial question, turn it inside out and upside down, and make the strange conclusion almost inevitable. From watching television day and night, Jimmy Jet starts to take on the characteristics of a TV set until "he grew a plug that looked like a tail."

Looking back

Looking at the world with a 'what if' attitude isolates cause-and-effect relationships in a direct way. For children, it's a natural way of looking at the world. They commonly pose any number of hypothetical questions to clarify and pinpoint what will happen under various eventualities. "What if it rains on Friday and I don't have my raincoat? Do I still have to go to school?" belongs to a clearly recognizable, although taxing, pattern of inquiry. Ironically, adults tend to lose patience with this kind of questioning and often ask children to 'stop asking so many questions' and 'start listening to the answers'. Adults see children pursuing tangents into the realm of imagination. Children, on the other hand, are just trying to figure out how things work.

9. ABCs and 1,2,3s

Many children come to school already able to recite the alphabet and count to ten. With sing-song rhymes ("The ABC Song" and "One, Two, Buckle My Shoe") and constant repetition, parents give their children a thorough introduction to the language and number systems. Given this early preparation, why are there so many alphabet and number books in primary classrooms and on library shelves? Indeed, why are alphabet books written at a junior or even adult level? *The Ultimate Alphabet Book* by Mike Wilks (New York, Henry Holt, 1986), for example, isn't meant for children at all. Two forces seem to be at work. One is that the concepts represented by mere recitation take a long time to develop. The other is that our fascination with this first initiation into the mystical rites of formal learning never leaves us. Since the attraction is so deep-rooted and of such long standing, it can be used to motivate related activities and learning.

In years past, this early learning was combined with the inculcation of prescriptive social values. Almost 300 years ago, children were taught in an alphabet poem that "In Adam's fall / We sinned all. / This life to mend / This book attend." The alphabet became a means to an end. Today, many contemporary pre-school and kindergarten books are actually written to facilitate both the rote learning of letters and numerals and the concepts behind them. When poetry is added, however, the purposes seem to change. The alphabet or numbers are often used as a springboard to achieve another goal. That goal might be to amuse or entertain, to help illuminate another aspect of learning, or to inculcate a social value. Whatever the goal, the vehicle is especially effective. Our life-long fascination with both

The 'Awful' A,B,Cs

A is for awful, **B** is for bad,
C is the worst cold I ever had.
D is for 'don't (and I hear *that* a lot!),
E is for everything I haven't got.

F stands for feelings, when they get hurt,
G are the grass-stains all over my shirt.
H is for headache, **I** is the ice
They put on my eye when I got punched twice.

J is the junk that was all I could see,
When my **K** for kite crashed into a tree!
L is for lousy, **M** is for mean,
N is how nasty all my friends have been.

O is for, "Oh, oh! I lost my key!"
P is the pocket where it was supposed to be.
Q is for quarrel, **R** is for rain,
S is how sad I'm feeling again.

T is the toothache that came in the night,
U is how ugly I look when I fight.
V is for villain, **W** is weird,
X marks the spot where my chicken pox appeared.

Y is for 'yelled at' and it wasn't much fun,
When my **Z** for zipper came undone.
So when I look back at this awful **ABC**,
The only thing not awful — is **me**!

the subject matter itself and the specialized form of language known as poetry makes the combination doubly powerful.

Theme starter (1): "The 'Awful' ABCs"

Just for fun, stop looking at the bright side of things for a moment and look at the 'awful' side. The immediate attraction in this poem is the novelty. Adults spend so much time trying to be positive for children, they sometimes forget that children can be gloomy, too, and for perfectly valid reasons. Children can relate personally to many of the situations listed, enjoy the irony of the standard rhythm and rhyme conveying the unusual content, and appreciate the upbeat ending. Introducing "The 'Awful' ABCs" right after a standard version increases the impact.

Some ABCs

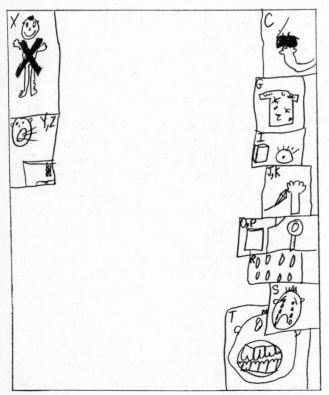

Christopher (age 8)

Follow-up suggestions for "The 'Awful' ABCs"

• With the poem on a transparency on the overhead projector, the children can follow along as the teacher reads aloud for the first few times. Volunteers can choose any letter they like and read the line containing that letter when it comes up in the reading. Eventually, the poem develops into a complete choral reading experience.

• With exposure to a variety of themes in alphabet books, children become familiar with the format and enjoy choosing a category for an original ABC and filling in the stems to match that category. This activity works best if a list of possible categories is first brainstormed. Suggestions range from seasonal themes to sports to television programs. As a class group or in smaller groups, they can then complete each letter with a word or phrase connected with the chosen theme. Once again, they should be encouraged to dispense with a rhyme scheme and find the most appropriate stems possible.

Activity palette — alphabet

• *Writing pattern books*

Base, Graeme. *Animalia*. Australia: Viking Kestrel, 1986; New York: Harry N. Abrams; Toronto: Irwin Publishing, 1987.

This gorgeously-drawn picture book offers a foreground illustrating an alliterative, often bizarre phrase, such as "Great green gorillas growing grapes in a gorgeous glass greenhouse." The background is rich in a complex montage of many smaller figures representing other words beginning with the same letter. While most primary children find many of the phrases too sophisticated to unlock on their own, they love to listen to them and then pore over the illustrations.

Once the alliterative pattern has been established, children are ready to write and illustrate their own picture book at their own level. A group book could be compiled by having each student choose one or two letters, and, if the book winds up with eight As and no Xs, everyone will be just as happy. Students can work together, pooling their ideas and sharing the tasks. Once a phrase, such as 'All the aliens are awful,' is selected, they can then illustrate the phrase and embed more 'A' words in the background.

Elting, Mary and Michael Folsom. *Q Is for Duck*. Illustrated by Jack Kent. New York: Houghton Mifflin, 1980.

This unique, alphabet guessing game raises prediction to an intriguing new level. After children have been exposed to the predictability of standard alphabet books, introduce them to "**A** is for Zoo / Why? / Because . . . **Animals** live in the zoo." Once they've explored the patterns and surprises of *Q Is for Duck* itself, children will be ready to create their own versions.

A is for Hallowe'en. Why? Because we bob for *apples* on Hallowe'en.
A is for paintings? Why? Because *artists* paint pictures.

If children have initial difficulty creating both parts of the statement, prepare some sample stems and let them complete the pattern.

A is for the Olympics. Why? . . .
B is for soccer. Why? . . .

- *Sculpting letters with plasticine*
Reid, Barbara. *Playing with Plasticine*. Toronto: Kids Can Press, 1988.

In the chapter entitled *For Keeps*, children are shown quite literally how to shape their ABCs from plasticine. Printed letters, joined printing, fancy letters, textured letters, name tags, and signs are included, as well as tips on making plasticine backgrounds and hanging up finished creations.

- *Responding through research*
After sharing *Applebet, an ABC*, make a list on chart paper of all the apple references children can supply from their own knowledge and all the questions about apples that the discussion may stimulate. Those questions can be used as a springboard into *The Amazing Apple Book* and the facts and activities waiting to be shared.

Bourgeois, Paulette. *The Amazing Apple Book*. Toronto: Kids Can Press, 1987.

As a follow-up to *Applebet, an ABC*, this book contains everything you would ever want to know about apples. Apples in history are detailed from Adam and Eve to Isaac Newton to Johnny Appleseed. The apple in pioneer times is explained, as well as how to make your own dried apples, apple cider, and apple vinegar. Even the life of the apple tree is covered from blossom to apple. When you add unusual apple facts, apple riddles, how to make apple dolls, apple yogurt, blue candy apples, and applewiches, *The Amazing Apple Book* can only be described as a comprehensive, stimulating, intriguing, and indispensible apple resource.

- *Writing a picture book with a buddy*

Alphabet picture books are ideal subjects for buddy-authoring projects. Older students are paired with younger students. Usually, the older student reads to the younger (although that pattern should be reversed if the younger student shows a desire to read) and, together, they discuss the various characteristics and enjoyable aspects of the book.

After a number of readaloud experiences in which alphabet books are the focus, the 'buddies' are encouraged to confer on the theme and content of a new picture book, conceived jointly and, depending on the age and experience of the younger child, carried out either jointly or by the older student. Story updating and revision conferences can be arranged, peer-revision and peer-editing components included, and contracts can even be made with accomplished student illustrators. At a publishing party at the conclusion of the unit, the new picture books are unveiled and read aloud by the authors.

Theme resource list — alphabet

- Merriam, Eve. *Hallowe'en ABC*. Illustrated by Lane Smith. New York: Macmillan, 1987.

Each letter begins a Hallowe'en word. Some choices are gleefully 'off the wall' and refreshingly original. All are enjoyable. The letter 'u', for example, begins the word 'umbrella'. What's the connection with Hallowe'en? The verse reveals that an umbrella would be useful when "It's raining pitchforks, / it's raining cats and dogs / and loathesome toadsome / bulging bullfrogs.'' Eve Merriam's tasteful word play is stylishly accompanied by a set of dramatic, imaginative drawings.

• Pilcher, Steve. *Elfabit*. Burlington, Ontario: Hayes Publishing, 1982.

Placing the alphabet in the context of the elfworld has two notable benefits. The vocabulary becomes exotic and playful and the text and drawings become interdependent. ''O is for ogre grumpy and fat. / P is for pixie taking his hat.'' Children respond enthusiastically to the imaginative creatures and depend on the visual context to make sense of and define the written clues. The illustrations are large, colorful, amusing, and beautifully rendered.

• Thornhill, Jan. *The Wildlife ABC, A Nature Alphabet*. Toronto: Greey de Pencier Books, 1988.

North American wildlife is realistically portrayed in the colorful illustrations accompanying the rhymes. The verses highlight particular aspects of an animal's life: ''E is for Eagle / Seeking salmon to eat. / F is for Frog with webbed hind feet.''

• Watson, Clyde. *Applebet, an ABC*. Illustrated by Wendy Watson. New York: Farrar, Straus, and Giroux, 1982.

The opening is an invitation to another world and another time: ''A is for apple as everyone knows. / Can you follow this one wherever it goes?'' Apple-picking, apple cider, an old-time rural fair, and a rural life that is no more make this ABC very much a history lesson. The autumn-tinged drawings capture the gentle wistfulness of the text.

Theme starter (2): ''Numbers''

Many young children are baffled by numbers of one sort or another. Since number concepts are acquired developmentally, anything past ten, at some stage, just become 'lotsa'. Imagine how a seven-digit telephone number must appear to some children. Indeed, as they labor patiently with counters over their 'times tables' or try to unravel the mysteries of 'gozintas' (e.g., two 'gozinta' four, twice), they often seem to be grappling with an impenetrable, alien language. The following poem was written to let children know that it's all right to be confused by numbers. Sooner or later, the important ones 'stick'.

Numbers

Around and around and around they spin,
A jumble of numbers with more popping in.
I don't know my phone number and I don't know my
   weight.
How in the world can I keep them all straight?

How many days in a week or hours in a day?
When I go to the store, how much should I pay?
I try to remember one way or another,
But the numbers come in one ear and go out the other.

In school, we add them and minus them, too.
We group them and times them and still we're not
   through.
"What would five apples cost?" my teacher demands.
I can't figure it out on the fingers of both hands!

Then, safe in my bed and just before sleep,
I see white, woolly shapes as I start counting sheep.
But there's one number I like, next day when I wake,
And I count up the candles on my birthday cake!

One Is a Pointer

One is a pointer that can also scratch your head.
(The index finger on one hand points and then scratches top of head.)

Two means you've won, with nothing being said.
(Index and second finger make a 'V for victory' sign.)

Three can salute, just to be polite.
(Thumb and little finger fold over palm, while the remaining three fingers are stretched out and held beside head in salute.)

Four is a dog that just might bite.
(Little finger is stretched out to join the index and next two fingers. The thumb remains folded over the palm. The little finger is moved to represent the mouth of a dog opening and closing.)

Five is an ear that waggles north and south.
(The thumb is raised from the palm to act as the waggling ear.)

Six is a stick in the playful dog's mouth.
(The index finger from the other hand is placed in the 'mouth'.)

Seven is a rabbit with ears one and two.
(A fist forms the head and the index and second fingers make the ears.)

Eight is a spider crawling up your shoe.
(Three fingers from one hand and four fingers and the thumb from the other are overlapped and spread to represent the legs of the spider.)

Nine came together with one unseen.
(The four fingers and thumb from one hand are interlocked with four fingers from the other hand. One thumb remains out of sight, folded inside a palm.)

Ten says, "Look! All my fingernails are clean!"
(The ten fingers are stretched out as if for inspection.)

Follow-up suggestions for "Numbers"

• For young people, birthdays are the most special of all days. For that reason alone, a monthly calendar displayed in the class-room is an essential item. At the beginning of each month, teachers print the names on the appropriate dates of children with birthdays that month. As the class keeps track of the pass-ing days, individual children and their friends have a way of figuring out how many more days there are until their birthday.

• As an individual activity, children share the numbers that are important or special in their lives. They might mention such num-bers as birthdates, addresses, lucky numbers, numbers of siblings, or their height. With just the numbers recorded under the child's name on chart paper, the list becomes an intriguing, individual, number profile. The profile could then be used for language experience purposes, prompting a variety of reading, discussion, or related writing activities. Children can always update or revise the profiles as they desire. For obvious reasons, however, personal telephone numbers should remain private information.

Response to "Numbers"

Alicia (age 7)

Activity palette — numbers

• *Sharing a number finger play*
See "One Is a Pointer" on page 92 and the general comments on finger play on page 27.

Theme resource list — numbers

• Bang, Molly. *Ten, Nine, Eight*. England: Penguin Books, 1987.

Countdown to bedtime becomes a warm and special time with rhymes such as "4 sleepy eyes which open and close and 3 loving kisses on cheeks and nose." The full-page illustrations are boldly drawn and richly colored, the happy result of adult skills applied with a childlike point of view. In this loving portrait of a father and young daughter at bedtime, stereotypes are neatly avoided.

• Demi. *Count the Animals, 1, 2, 3*. New York: Grosset and Dunlap, 1986.

Most counting books stop at either ten or twelve. Demi's book is unusual in that it goes all the way to twenty. Since, during the early primary years, the number concepts beyond ten are still forming, Demi's book offers a valuable and entertaining perspective on those concepts. The illustrations are bright, bold, and totally charming. The verses that accompany the numbers, such as "These rabbits may / be hard to count, / but fourteen is / the right amount," are easy to read and appropriate.

• Grossman, Virginia. *Ten Little Rabbits*. Illustrated by Sylvia Long. San Francisco: Chronicle Books, 1991.

This picture book is a marvelous antidote to the 'ten little Indians' stereotype that comes down to children through counting rhymes. In this number book, rabbits portray the culture of traditional North American Indian life. As the text says, "Three busy messengers sending out the news," the characters are grouped around a signal fire. This scene is followed by "Four clever trackers looking for some clues." The illustrations are rich in detail and warmly rendered.

• Ockenga, Stan and Eileen Doolittle. *World of Wonders, A Trip Through Numbers*. Boston: Houghton Mifflin, 1988.

World of Wonders connects counting and collecting. Each number from one to twelve is represented by a full-page photograph of an eclectic, jam-packed collection of figures, artifacts, and objects with literary or cultural significance. The fun for children lies in treating each page as a treasure hunt for numbers. As they start with the number one, "The ringmaster calls from far away. / 'Come one, come all,' he seems to say. / 'There is a wondrous world around us / And countless creatures who'll astound us." For the most part, since the vocabulary and allusions are often sophisticated, the poetry should definitely be treated as readaloud material.

Looking back

With any thematic unit, one question always comes up, "How long should children work with these activities?" Since this particular unit includes suggestions for some relatively long-term, 'buddy' activities, the question is even more crucial. The answer depends solely of the success of the unit and the teacher's observation of the children. When children have had enough, they will let you know. Continuing beyond that stage, even if the activities are worthwhile, is pointless. Even when collaborating with older children from another class, if the younger children are asking, "Do we have to work with them again today?" it's time for a rest. Conversely, if the activities are going well, concluding before the children are ready will short-circuit a valuable learning experience. Whatever is substituted invariably falls flat. When children are finished with a unit before teachers think they should be, teachers start talking about short attention spans. When children are intrinsically interested in what they're doing, they can continue all day. Teachers need to read the signs and let the children determine how long a unit should be.

10. Sound

The celebration of sound in all its manifestations is gradually assuming its rightful place in school curricula. For too long, even sound in the form of listening and speaking was neglected in favor of the supposedly separate and more important tasks of learning to read and write. Now that we've come to appreciate to some degree the truly integrated nature of language, we are beginning to realize how crucial oral and aural experiences are to the development of reading and writing skills. Reading aloud to children, for example, is now an essential component of any language arts program at the elementary level. The inherent link between talking and thinking has also generated demands for 'talk-driven' curricula in all subject areas.

In a broader sense, exploring and making use of sound assists and directs much of our learning and our expression of that learning. The full spectrum of sound offers a rich context, invaluable clues, and unique inspiration as we try to make sense of our world and our lives. From the coarse rumbling of a bus, the sudden barking of a dog, or the faint rustling of wind through leaves, the world around us is a complex and shifting matrix of noises. At another point in the spectrum, when we organize sound by pitch and rhythmical pattern, we encounter music. Once again, with music, we discover an inextricable link with young children's language. Nursery rhymes, such as "Three Blind Mice," "Ring Around the Rosie," and "Mary Had a Little Lamb," are enshrined in melody. Lullabies and skipping songs are passed on from generation to generation. Even learning the ABCs is facilitated with song.

All our myriad thoughts about and feeling for sound converge

Rock 'n' Roll Chant

K-boom-boom-boom-boom
Big drum meets
K-thoom-thoom-thoom-thoom
Bass guitar beats

K-wang-ang-ang-ang
Heavy-metal whine
Of a rock 'n' roll trio
Out to have a good time

K-boom-ang-thoom-ang
Do what you dare
As the lead singer shrieks
And leaps in the air

K-wang-ang-ang-ang
Loud and bright
Rock 'n' roll music
Makes me feel all right

K-boom-ang-thoom-ang
Dance with your friends
K-thoom-ang-boom-bang
As this song ends

in poetry. As well as being about sound and the role sound plays in our lives, poetry itself can be crafted carefully and elevated to the realm of song. Poetry as both sound and music can lead us to a better understanding of language and life. For these reasons, the poems and activities that follow encourage children to investigate their world not with new eyes, but with new ears.

Theme starter: "Rock 'n' Roll Chant"

Neil Young wrote the prophetic words, "Hey, hey, my, my. Rock and roll will never die." The revolutionary music that shocked and threatened one generation is now the mainstream music of another. Children experience and respond to rock music at an early age and are never too young to explore and enjoy what it's all about. With "Rock 'n' Roll Chant," children enjoy the sound effects that represent each instrument, the light, up-tempo, carefree tone, and the stereotypical portrait of a rock group on stage. In a small way, they also have an opportunity to explore the sound and function of the instruments used in a rock trio.

Sound

Ian (age 7)

Follow-up suggestions for "Rock 'n' Roll Chant"

• When children have heard the poem a few times, they are ready to take part in a choral-speaking performance. With the poem on an overhead projector or the sound lines copied out on chart paper, individuals or pairs can recite the instrumental parts when cued by the teacher. The large group recites the rest of the text. The reverse works equally well. Teachers sometimes split the large group into three, assign each one a different instrument (drum, bass guitar, lead guitar) and, with hand signals, conduct their own musical variation.

• In discussion with the children, elicit the names of as many other musical instruments as they know. For each one, have them invent a word approximation of the sound, such as the "K-wang-ang-ang-ang" of the electric guitar in the poem. With these words on an overhead projector or chart paper, volunteers can perform each instrument on cue as the teacher conducts the 'orchestra'.

Activity palette

• *Creating water-chime songs*

First, fill five tumblers or glass containers with varying amounts of water. When struck with a spoon, each glass rings with a different tone. A little experimentation will produce five distinct and pleasing tones.

Next, choose a subject for a song, such as "sunshine," from suggestions offered by the children. Brainstorm a list of words associated with that subject and choose four of the suggestions for the first song. These words and the subject are printed on cards and one card is placed beside each of the water-chime glasses.

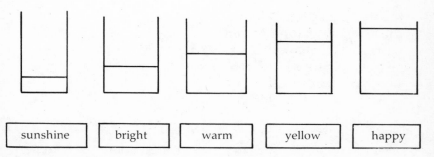

| sunshine | bright | warm | yellow | happy |

Children create songs by tapping on a glass as many times as they like, while reciting the appropriate word beside it. A sample song might be "Sunshine. Warm, warm. Bright. Yellow, yellow. Sunshine. Happy. Sunshine." A different, random combination creates a different song. The variations are considerable. By changing the subject and the associated words, completely new songs can be created. As they become familiar with the experience, children will spontaneously begin to sing as they match the tone of their voices to the tones of the tumblers.

• *Making sound associations*

Many teachers create a listening activity in which children guess the identity of a number of sound effects. These effects are either pre-recorded on tape or produced on the spot while the children 'hide their eyes'. The sound effects usually produce a varied, impressionistic impact. Depending on their past experiences and willingness to freely associate, children will often come up with any number of perfectly valid answers to each sound challenge. If teachers label these associations as 'wrong', they will be misleading and discouraging their children. If one were to rattle a large piece of bristol board, for example, would the 'correct' answer be "thunder" or "bristol board"?

Far better to ask children what each sound reminds them of. These associations can be printed on chart paper as each sound is produced. Teachers should feel free to model the process by adding their own associations from time to time. When the actual identity of the sound effect is revealed, the true, open-ended nature of guessing is also revealed. A specific sound effect can be produced in a specific way and yet still give rise to multiple, valid associations.

Here are a few suggestions for sound effects to initiate the activity:
— tearing of paper or cloth
— clicking of a ball-point pen
— wrinkling of cellophane, newsprint, or tinfoil
— fast movement of a thumb across the teeth of a comb
— sandpaper on wood
— blowing across the top of an empty pop bottle.

• *Categorizing sounds*

Either in a large group or in small groups operating independently, direct the children to brainstorm a list of sounds and who or what makes each sound. Give them a few, totally diverse examples to demonstrate how open-ended the activity can be. For example, pencils scratch, cows moo, and a person coughs.

When the lists are complete or the children start to 'run down,' divide the children into small groups and ask them to put sounds together that belong together in a new, separate list. Each list should have a title that explains why those sounds are together.

loud sounds

car honking
door slamming
bell ringing
principal shouting
motor running

When the lists are compared, the children will recognize that crossovers have occurred. Sounds categorized in one way can also be categorized in another. From these lists, children can be encouraged to come up with all-new categories and mix and match sounds from all the lists into entirely new ones.

• *Cataloguing sounds*
The poem "Barnyard Chat" by Stephanie Calmenson (see *Theme resource list*), is composed entirely of animal sounds, such as 'quack', 'meow', 'oink', and 'moo'. Similar lists can be created by suggesting categories and assisting children to brainstorm appropriate sounds for each category. When completed, the lists can be displayed in the classroom for reference when the children are reading, writing, storytelling, or discussing. These categories might include the following:

animal sounds
earth, air, fire, and water sounds
sounds people make
machine sounds.

One such catalogue might look like this:

sounds people make

sneeze, cough, talk
yell, shout, cry
whistle, snort, snap fingers
stamp feet, laugh, howl,
giggle, groan, sing.

- *Building a 'jug' band*

A 'jug' band is a small folk music or jazzband that uses such instruments as harmonicas and kazoos to carry melody and home-made instruments (jugs, washboards, washtubs) for percussive effects.

A jug band is relatively easy to assemble. A list of some of the possible home-made instruments follows. These suggestions can be augmented by a few of the simple instruments found in most schools, such as hand drums, tambourines, wood blocks, and xylophones. For the purposes of a jug band, xylophones should be left with only the notes of the pentatonic scale. These notes can then be played in any order and still produce an attractive and harmonious pattern.

Jug band instruments:

drum: a large, empty cardboard carton turned upside down and struck with a wooden ruler

shaker: an empty milk container with a handful of pebbles or beads inside

elastic guitar: a piece of wood with an elastic strung tightly across two nails (several elastics of differing thicknesses can be strung side by side)

tissue paper and comb: paper folded once over comb and hummed through

bottle bass: sound obtained by blowing directly and gently across the top of a large, empty bottle

water chimes: tumblers or glass containers with varying amounts of water inside; strike with a spoon to produce a tone.

Begin with a song everyone knows, such as "Row, Row, Row Your Boat" or "Miss Mary Mack." Start with the rhythm instruments, one by one, add the melody in the same manner, and introduce the xylophone in a pentatonic pattern for coloring.

Theme resource list

• Bauer, Caroline Feller, ed. *Rainy Day Poems*. Illustrated by Michelle Chessare. New York: J.B. Lippincott, 1986.

"KA-TRUM" by Byrd Baylor. The sound of pounding rain, "KA-TRUM, KA-TRUM, KA-TRUM," stimulates an imagined scene of another kind of pounding from past times: "When buffalo run / They darken the sun. / They cover the sky / When they pass by." Indian hunters enter the scene and an entire, unique drama springs into life through sounds and rhythms.

• Brewton, Sara; John E. Brewton; and John Brewton Blackburn (editors). *Of Quarks, Quasars, and Other Quirks*. New York: Thomas Y. Crowell, 1977.

With the all-pervading influence of television, children have difficulty visualizing life without television let alone developing an objective viewpoint on its pros and cons. The following poems should stimulate some useful discussion.

"The Day the T.V. Broke" by Gerald Jones. The unthinkable occurs. "It was awful. / First, / the silence. I thought I'd die." When the silence is broken as the house "began to speak," the irony rapidly mounts. For children, this inside-out point of view is as challenging as a puzzle.

"Tee-Vee Enigma" by Selma Raskin. Many people have a love/hate relationship with television. "We jeer / And we sneer — / And continue / To peer." Our inconsistencies regarding television are concisely pinpointed in this cleverly-constructed poem. "Tee-Vee Enigma" offers a natural entry into an exploration of how television affects our lives.

• Cole, Joanna and Calmenson, Stephanie, ed. *The Read-Aloud Treasury*. Illustrated by Ann Schweninger. New York: Doubleday, 1988.

"Barnyard Chat" by Stephanie Calmenson. Composed entirely of animal sounds, "Barnyard Chat" is a rollicking, choral-speaking treat. Fifteen sounds, such as 'honk', 'oink', and 'moo,' are represented in this rhyming, animal singalong. By assigning a couple of children to each sound, a class can become an instant barnyard symphony.

- Ireson, Barbara, ed. *Verse That Is Fun*. London: Faber and Faber, 1962.

"Song of the Pop-Bottles" by Morris Bishop. This ever-popular tongue-twister begins "Pop-bottles, pop-bottles in pop shops" and ends with an inevitable "pop!" In between is a lot of pure, giggling fun.

- McCord, David. *One at a Time*. Boston: Little, Brown, 1977.

"Song of the Train" is a "clickety-clack" of "wheels on the track." Starting with a slow and deliberate "click-ety-clack" and with an ever-increasing tempo, the poem offers a simple, direct, and vivid sound portrait. Choral speaking emerges spontaneously.

- Merriam, Eve. *Jamboree*. New York: Dell, 1984.

"Kitty Cornered." What happens when a child wants to stroke a cat and "Grrrrrr. The kitten doesn't want to play, / not today"? This gentle but noisy drama is played out with a host of sounds and tones. Children love to join in on the pssts, purrs, grrs, and meows.

"The Baby-Sitter and the Baby." Even from the title and the opening lines, "Hush hush hush the baby-sitter sighs / waw! waw! waw! the little baby cries," the conflict is clear. Since each character is represented by different and distinctive sounds, vocal tones, and attitudes, the poem ideally suits a two-voice reading. Children enter very quickly into the baby's uninhibited role.

"Ululation." The lines, "With a chuck, cluck, clack, / With a hum, gobble, quack," include only a few of the 45 different sound words used in this poem. Associating the various sounds with an appropriate animal (or human) flows naturally from hearing the poem.

- Moore, Lilian. *See My Lovely Poison Ivy*. New York: Atheneum, 1977.

"Why." The simple "tickety-tick" of the clock by day is transformed into a "TOCKETY-TOCKETY-TOCK-TOCK-TOCK" in the dark of night. Children learn the poem quickly and delight in the rhythm and sounds.

Looking back

One sound not mentioned in this unit is the predominant sound in many classrooms — the teacher talking. In questionnaires about teacher talk filled out by teachers, they state overwhelmingly that they believe wholeheartedly in a talk-driven curriculum and that the children do most of the talking in their classrooms. In most observational reviews of classroom practice, however, the opposite is usually found to be true.

This unit offers teachers an opportunity to review their own practice. Some teachers tape themselves over a two- or three-day period, some use videotape, and still others collaborate with a trusted colleague and sit in on each other's lessons. They then compare how much they are talking and the kinds of talking they're doing with the ideal they have in mind. If the gap between their intended and actual practice is wider than they're comfortable with, they can devise ways to refine their approach. Teachers find it refreshing and reassuring to periodically take the pulse of their current practice and discover if it truly is consistent with their own beliefs and intentions.

11. Setting up an activity-based environment

Based on beliefs

When teachers organize their classrooms as activity-based, learning-centre environments, they are affirming specific beliefs about children as learners. The classroom environment becomes an extension of those beliefs. These teachers believe that children need to be actively involved in the learning process, taking responsibility for and making many of the decisions related to their own learning. Since they believe that children need to interact with their peers as they learn, small-group, cooperative learning is a mainstay of their programs. At the same time, they also believe that children need time and encouragement to reflect on what and how they learn.

At the heart of all these beliefs about learning is the conviction that learning happens best in a language-based, talk-driven curriculum. The foundation of that curriculum is built on cooperation for the good of all and respect for self and others. In a contemporary, learning/teaching environment, children and adults learn together in an environment free of sexist, social, and cultural stereotypes.

Basic components

Some teachers organize their entire program around learning centres, while others incorporate them only for part of each day. Regardless of how long they are used, all students must take part when they are used. Reserving learning centres just for those students who finish their regular work early or just for enrichment activities violates the very beliefs about learning that necessitated this kind of approach in the first place. If children are receiving mixed messages about the value of learning centres, the effectiveness of the approach is neutralized.

Flexibility is the key to setting up the program. To facilitate a learning-centre approach, teachers need to organize their day in a flexible and integrated manner; the furniture should be arranged flexibly to accommodate work and movement patterns; and the centres themselves should be constantly evaluated, renewed, and adjusted to match children's interests and to offer concrete experiences and opportunities for problem-solving.

Equipment checklist

Equipment to support a learning-centre approach would include items such as the following:

— carpets (mats, cushions)
— water table
— easels (for painting and chart paper)
— manipulative materials for creating and exploring (Lego, attribute and pattern blocks, etc.)
— typewriter
— aquarium
— access to VCR and television
— commercial puppets
— musical instruments (tambourine, xylophone, etc.)

— sand table
— big blocks
— filmstrip projector
— cassette recorder with headphones and microphone
— access to word processor
— overhead projector
— terrarium (plants, rocks, shells, etc.)

Learning centres

While some learning centres are set up on an ad hoc basis to stimulate and support a specific unit, theme, or mode of inquiry, some centres should be considered as permanent classroom fixtures. A selection could be made from the following:

Big blocks
— a variety of sizes
— ramps, ladders
— boxes for storage

Cut-and-paste centre
— variety of disposable magazines for photomontage and collage
— colored construction paper
— stir sticks, pipe cleaners, straws, wool, aluminum foil, cotton balls
— 'found' materials (boxes, cartons, cardboard, bits of material)
— tape, glue, stapler, scissors, rulers

Manipulative centre
— commercial, interlinked products such as Lego, Tinker Toys

Mathematics centre
— measuring tapes, rulers, metre sticks, trundle wheel, string
— personal scale, balance scale, variety of weights
— attribute and pattern blocks, Multilink, counters

Media centre
— filmstrip viewers
— cassette recorder with headphones and microphone
— access to VCR and television
— overhead projector

Modeling centre
— clay, plasticine in various colors
— hard, covered surfaces on which to work
— modeling tools, such as stir sticks

Painting and illustrating centre
— paints, a variety of brushes
— paper in a variety of sizes and colors
— easels
— crayons, oil pastels, pencil crayons, colored chalk, sketching charcoal, colored markers

Puppet centre
— varied, commercial puppets, hand-made puppets
— small, fold-up puppet stage

Reading centre
— picture books (a large selection of individual titles)

- wordless picture books
- 'big' books
- children's novels (a large selection of individual titles)
- poetry books
- information books (on a wide variety of subjects and themes)
- anthologies
- books on audio-cassette tape for assisted reading
- student-written material
- dictionaries, thesauri, atlases (a few copies of different editions)
- magazines, newspapers, comic books
- functional books (catalogues, recipe books, television guide)

Sand table
- digging tools, spoons
- variety of containers with varied capacities

Science centre
- magnifying glass
- microscope
- terrarium
- aquarium
- shells, rocks, plants
- reference books (animals, birds, insects, rocks and minerals, weather, astronomy)

Water table
- variety of containers with varied capacities
- objects that sink and float

Writing centre
- writing tools (pens, pencils, markers, crayons)
- writing paper (blank, lined, newsprint, white, colored, various sizes)
- notebooks (blank, ready-made, variety of sizes and shapes, scrapbooks, journals)
- experience chart paper and easel
- writing folders
- access to word processor and/or typewriter
- accessories (stapler, tape, scissors, rulers)

Index of activities

Although the scope of response activities in this book is wide and varied, no single theme contains them all. An activity from one theme, however, can often be adapted for use with another. Teachers may also decide to cross over themes to highlight certain activities or to satisfy an individual's desire for further research topics. For these reasons, the following index traces each particular type of activity throughout the book.

Construction, 31, 32, 61, 63, 102
Choral speaking, 40, 61, 69, 87, 99
Discussion groups, 21, 32, 40, 50, 63, 69, 77, 87, 99, 100
Finger play, 27, 28, 92, 94
Illustration, 27, 61, 71, 72, 77, 87, 89
Measuring, 50
Mobiles, 71
Painting, 63
Photomontage and collage, 21, 52
Plasticine, 31, 40, 55, 70, 88
Research, 21, 33, 55, 66, 71, 88
Role play, 21 27, 32, 42, 50
Storytelling, 43, 77
Sand, 80
Water, 19, 80
Writing activities, 19, 20, 21, 32, 40, 41, 50, 53, 79, 93, 99, 101
Writing stories, 42, 52, 79, 87, 89

Glossary

The definitions in this selected glossary reflect the meanings used in the text.

brainstorming: generating a list of examples, ideas, or questions to illustrate, expand, or explore a central idea or topic (record all ideas; no evaluating of ideas during collecting; quantity of ideas is important; encourage students to expand on each other's ideas; "zany" ideas are welcome).

child-centred: an approach to learning in which the developmental needs of the child determine how instruction is organized; the program adapts to the child rather than the reverse.

choral speaking: a group speaking/reading aloud; for effect, the voices of individuals or small groups are often used in counterpoint to the main group.

conferencing: discussing ideas and problems in pairs or small groups; conferences can be conducted in a variety of formats with and without the teacher.

co-operative learning: a variety of small-group instructional techniques focusing on peer collaboration.

language experience: an integrated approach to language development in which an individual's or group's own words are written down as presented and then used as the basis for instruction in reading, writing, listening, and speaking.

learning centre: a space in the classroom designated for activities involving a specific medium (e.g., plasticine), specialized equipment (e.g., big blocks), mode of presentation (e.g., puppets), or specialized area of study (e.g., mathematics); a learning centre is designed to stimulate and facilitate 'hands-on' investigation of concepts. Learning or activity centres are associated with and are meant to support child-centred, activity-based programs.

poetry: crafting and sculpting language, often in metrical form and rhyme, to create in as vivid, direct, and personally significant a way as possible a specific effect on a listener or reader.

readalouds: any material read aloud, usually by the teacher; students of all ages should be read to regularly; readalouds should comprise both fiction and non-fiction and should be drawn from a variety of genres.

scribing: transcribing the words of another; acting as a 'scribe'.

story: with young children, the sense that the function of language predominates over form; whether orally or in written form, children should tell what they need to tell in their own way without worrying unduly about specific formats set aside for fiction, non-fiction, poetry, or prose.

storytelling: an oral tradition in which the structure and substance of a story is memorized, but not the exact words. Stories may include legend, oral lore, wonder tales, stories about how and why, epic narrative, and personal history.

webbing: a commonly-used method of graphically linking and organizing associated concepts, thoughts, symbols, and related activities.

whole language: a learning/teaching approach that emphasizes the integration of language 'threads' (i.e., listening, speaking, reading, writing, thinking) within the context of meaningful communication (e.g., a single writing task may engage a student in a range of discussion, composing, editing/revising, reading tasks); includes the idea of moving away from isolated, fragmented approaches such as a regular 'grammar' period outside the context of the writing process.